BEGINNING BULLETIN BOARDS
BASIC SKILLS
HANDS-ON WALL, TABLE, AND FLOOR ACTIVITIES

by Bonnie Mertzlufft, Brenda Morton, Virginia Woolf
illustrated by Marilynn G. Barr

Publisher: Roberta Suid
Editor: Carol Whiteley
Production: Susan Cronin-Paris

monday morning.

Monday Morning is a registered trademark of
Monday Morning Books, Inc.

ISBN 1-878279-05-X

Printed in the United States of America

9 8 7 6 5 4 3 2

Contents

Introduction

The hardest lesson in school shouldn't be sitting still and quiet. Young children need to move, even in the classroom. But they also need to learn. Beginning Bulletin Boards: Basic Skills is designed to provide you with a supplemental program that fosters active learning. The activities in the book, aimed at kindergarten and first grade children, reinforce and review basic skills through manipulative bulletin board work, reproducibles, worksheets, and take-home activities.

Four characters—Charlie, a cuddly rabbit; Baxter, an adventurous, red-headed boy; Penny, an active girl who lives on a farm; and Bashful, a shy teddy bear—are each a consistent theme through one section of the book. The characters are vivid, with friendly, fun-loving personalities, but they need the children's help in every activity. For example, in one activity, Charlie, the pink rabbit, has gotten lost. Patterns showing Charlie and several rabbit friends are mounted on the bulletin board, with Charlie appearing in different ordinal positions. The children are directed to find Charlie in each pattern by hanging up a label with the correct ordinal number of his position.

Additional activities and homework throughout the book give extra practice in particular skill work. For example, after the children have found Charlie in each pattern strip of rabbits, they can continue working on their ordinal number skills by completing two worksheets. The first worksheet asks them to color a shape in a particular position in a row; the second worksheet directs them to indicate if Charlie is located in first or last position.

Each theme section provides everything you need: teacher notes, patterns, reproducibles, plus complete directions and illustrations. A materials list is provided below.

We use the ideas in the book in a number of ways:

1. to introduce a topic to the whole group
2. as small-group reinforcement
3. for individual practice
4. for individual testing

Please remember that if you use the activities as lessons, the concepts involved must be introduced and taught before the children can be expected to work on the activities alone.

Making the Bulletin Boards

We encourage you to make the bulletin boards as attractive and appealing as possible. You can do this by using bright colors and interesting materials and by adding the borders and corners shown on the illustrations. You can make titles for the boards using letter patterns you cut out, or you can use stencils.

Patterns can be cut out from several different materials:

1. different colors of construction paper

2. tagboard or poster board

3. wallpaper samples

You will also need a few standard items for the activities: felt-tip pens, colored pencils or crayons, rubber cement, library pockets, pushpins, yarn, tape, rope, straight pins, paper clips, stapler, hole punch, and scissors (a few activities call for other basics, such as strips of Velcro; specific materials for each activity are found on the Teacher Notes pages). Plastic bags make good containers for storing bulletin board pieces, or you may want to provide cloth or net bags. All bulletin board pieces should be laminated for durability.

There are several ways children can place answer pieces in position:

1. They can hang a hole-punched answer piece on a straight pin or a pushpin.

2. You can attach a yarn loop to each answer piece and have the children put it over a pushpin.

3. You can make hooks on the pieces by pushing a bent paper clip through each piece and taping it in the back.

4. You can staple the permanent pieces to the bulletin board, leaving a slot for the children to slip in the answer pieces.

5. You can string up a clothesline and let the children hang the answers on it with paper clips or clothespins.

Pattern enlargements can be made in two ways. If you have access to a copy machine with enlarging and reducing capabilities, that will do the trick. If not, you can use the copy machine to copy the figure onto a special transparency and then use the overhead projector to enlarge it.

Using the Bulletin Boards

When the children work on a bulletin board activity, encourage them to get involved: hang up answer patterns, drop answer patterns in pockets, think, review skills, move around, think some more, try again. In other words, encourage them to have fun while they learn. If you want several children to work at the bulletin board at the same time, you can provide them with several sets of answer patterns, each set made in a different color paper. Children can hang the answers next to each other, and you can easily determine which child used which color. If an answer is wrong, you'll be able to work individually with the child, then have him or her try again. *Note: If you do not have access to bulletin boards, use a table or the floor.*

We hope that you'll enjoy making and using these bulletin board activities as much as we have. We're certain you'll find that the time you spend preparing them will reap great benefits in the classroom, both in skills learned and in activity enjoyed.

Bonnie Mertzlufft

Brenda Morton

Virginia Woolf

This is Charlie. Charlie is a large pink rabbit who can do a lot of amazing things. The skills Charlie teaches through his bulletin board activities are:

1. Left and right
2. Measuring
3. Alphabet matching
4. Ordinal numbers

Charlie Rabbit Pattern

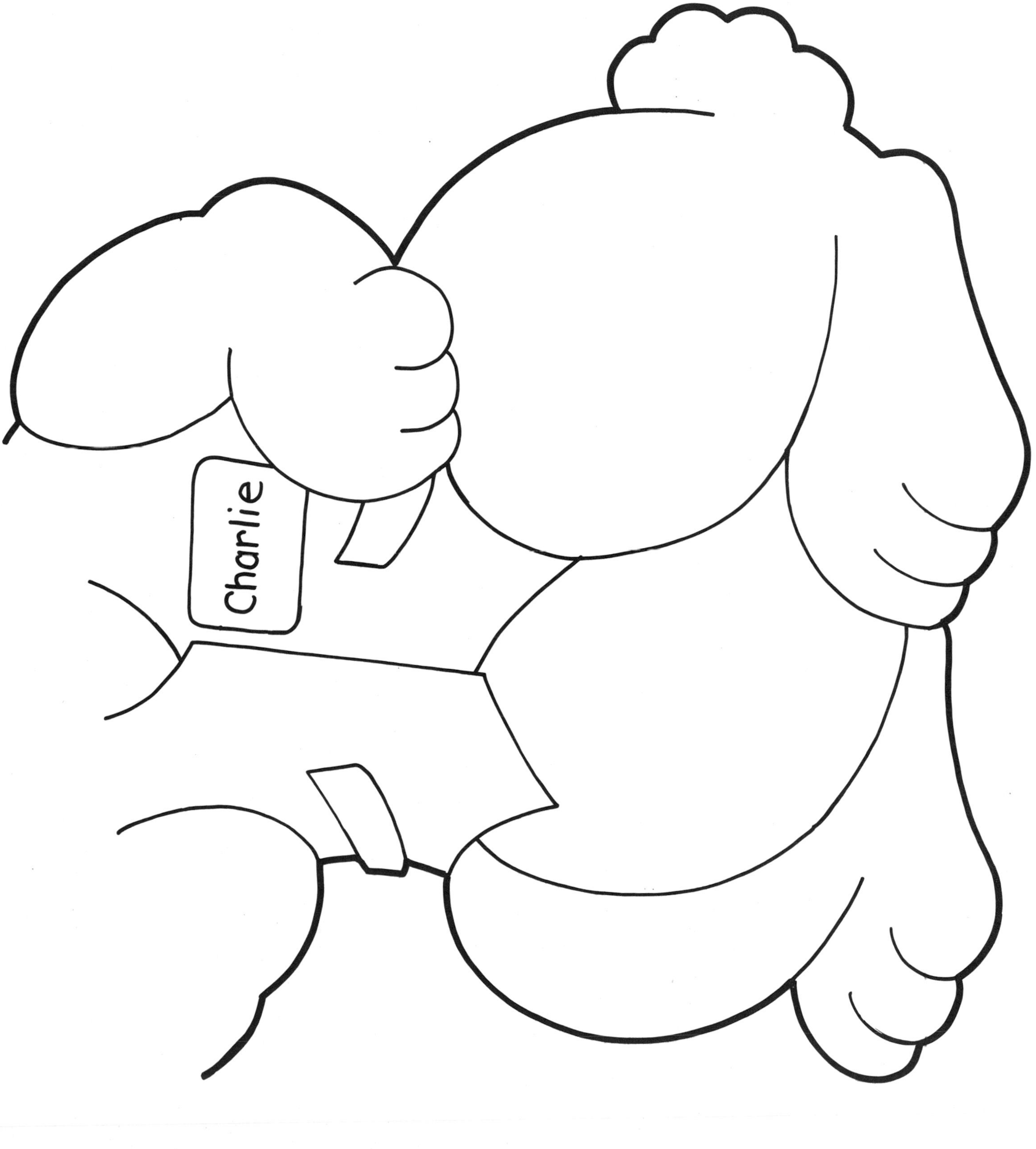
Charlie

Activity 1: Which Way for Charlie?

Objective: To recognize Charlie in left and right positions

Materials: Patterns, pink and other color crayons, scissors, pink and other colors of construction paper, felt-tip pen, hole punch, pushpins, plastic bag, stapler

Construction: Enlarge and duplicate a Charlie pattern from pink construction paper. Duplicate and cut out a left and a right hand pattern. Mount Charlie to the center of the board and place the left hand pattern on his left, the right hand pattern to his right. Then duplicate and cut out the Charlie and friend pattern cards. Color the rabbit over the tab on each card pink—this is Charlie—and the other rabbit in each card—the friend—a different color. Mount the cards on the board. Place a pin on each tab. Duplicate and cut out six "Left" tags and seven "Right" tags (the extra tag will keep the last choice from being obvious). Punch a hole in the top of each tag. Laminate all the tags and store them in a plastic bag pinned to the board. Decorate the board and put up the title "Which Way for Charlie?"

Directions: Review the concept of left and right with the children. Then explain to the children that they will be looking for Charlie, the pink rabbit, in a number of cards on the board. If they find Charlie on the right in a card, they should hang a tag that says "Right." If Charlie is on the left, they should hang up a card that says "Left." Have the children hang up the correct tag under each Charlie and friend card. Then check their work.

Variation: Make color tags, or color word tags for older children, that match the colors of Charlie's friends. Have the children hang the correct color tag under each card.

Worksheets: You can vary the first worksheet by having the children color the cars facing right red and the cars facing left blue.

Books to Read Aloud: Left and Right by Li Zigan; The Look Again... & Again, & Again Book by Beau Gardener; My Hands by Aliki; Hand, Hand, Fingers, Thumb by Al Perkins; All About Hands by Elizabeth E. Watson.

Charlie and Friend Patterns

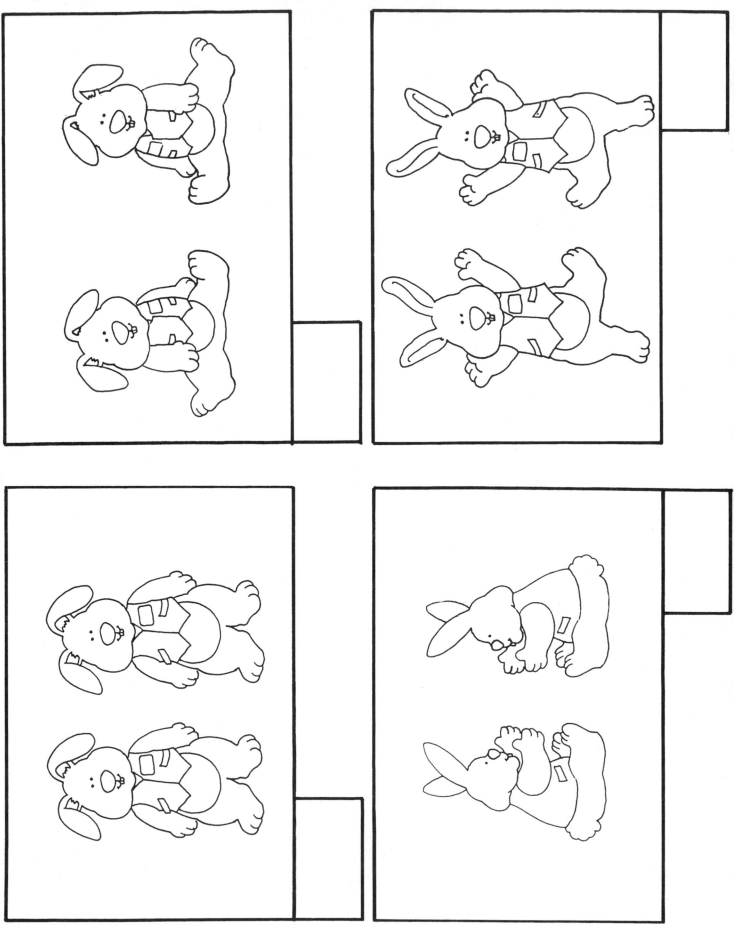

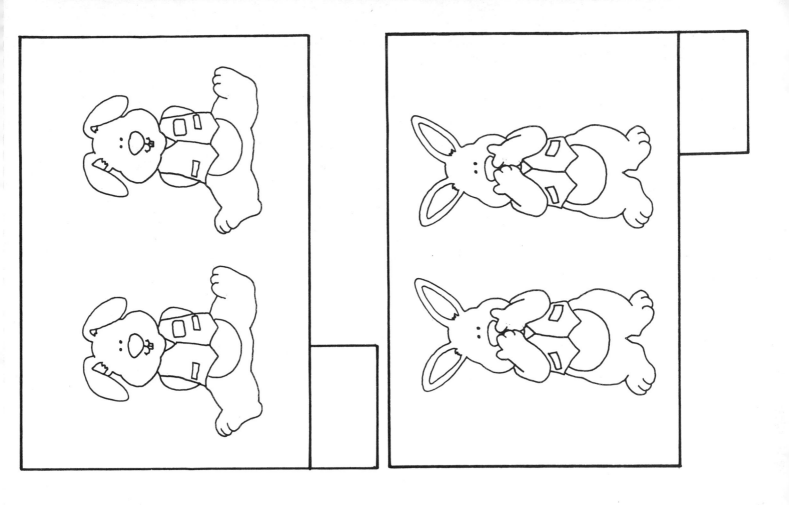

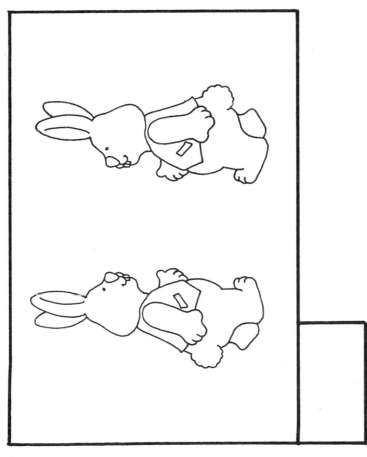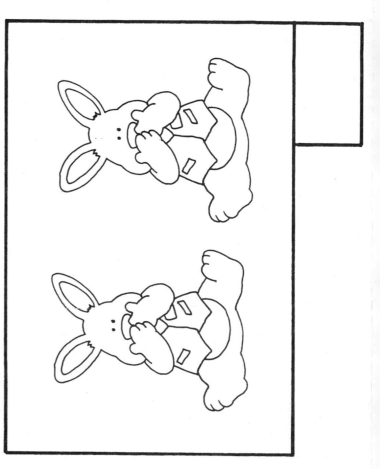

Hand and Tag Patterns

Name _____

Write L in each truck facing left.　　　　　　Write R in each truck facing right.

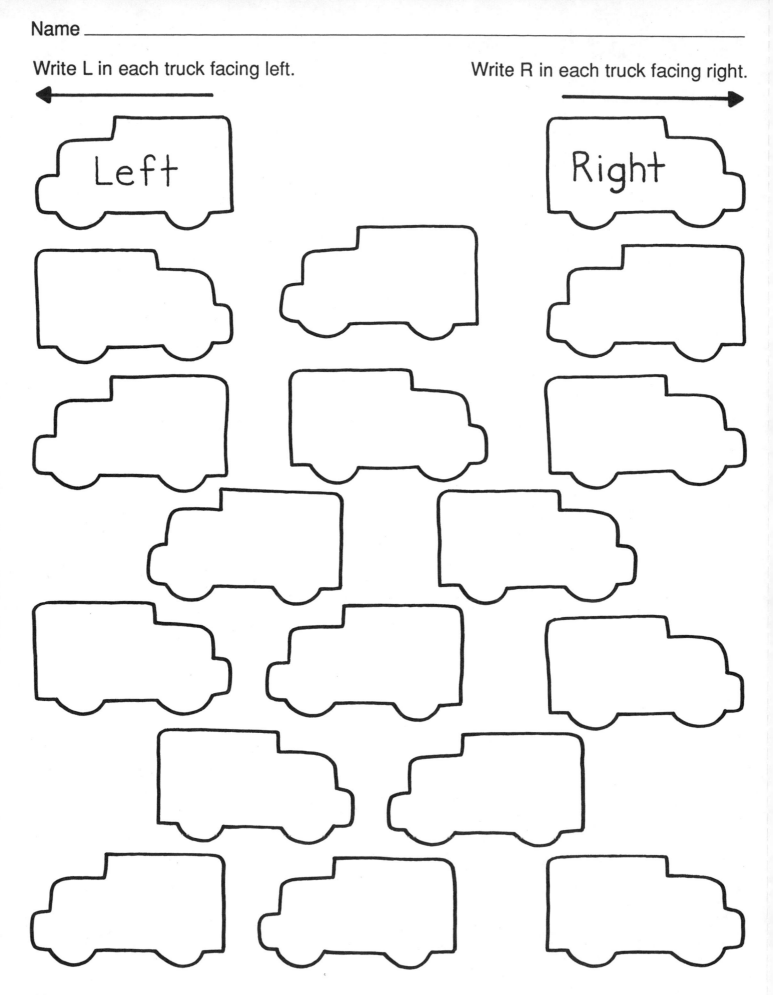

　　　　　　　　　　© 1990 Monday Morning Books, Inc.

Name _____

Color each arrow pointing right red.
Color each arrow pointing left blue

_____'s Homework

Dear Parents,

    To help reinforce the concept of left and right, take a walk with your child in an open outdoor space. Take 10 steps, then stop and ask your child to turn left. Go 10 more steps and have your child turn to the right. Continue walking, alternating left and right turns. Later, in the space below, have your child draw a picture of some of the things he or she saw along the way. Return the paper to school.

Our Path

Start Here

Charlie's Measuring

Worksheets

Activity 2: Charlie's Measuring

Objective: To match paper rulers to different carrot lengths

Materials: Patterns, scissors, felt-tip pen, orange, green, white, and pink construction paper, hole punch, pushpins, pocket folder, worksheet, stapler, paste or glue stick

Construction: Enlarge and duplicate the Charlie pattern from pink construction paper and mount it on the board. Duplicate and cut out from the orange paper one each of the carrot patterns. Duplicate and cut out 10 carrot tops from green paper, adjusting the size to suit the different-size carrots. Glue the carrots to the green tops and number the carrots from 1 to 10 in random order. Mount the carrots on the board. Then, out of white paper, make a paper ruler the same length as each of the carrots. Be sure the ruler is the same length as the orange part of the carrot only. Mark off the rulers and then put a number on each that tells the number of inches that ruler is. Punch a hole in the top of each ruler and laminate all of them. Then hang the rulers on the board. Run off the appropriate number of the following worksheet and place the worksheets in a pocket folder attached to the board. Decorate the bulletin board and mount the title "Charlie's Measuring."

Directions: Discuss paper rulers with the children and how to use them. Then explain that Charlie is getting ready to take his carrots to the fair. He wants to take only the biggest ones. Direct the students to measure each carrot on the board by matching a ruler to it that is the same length. Have each student record the carrot lengths on a worksheet. At the end of the activity, check the students' work.

Worksheets: The second worksheet requires centimeter rulers. The third worksheet requires scissors and paste.

Parent Letter: Use the carrots the students bring in from their homework assignment for one of the following activities:

1. Cut the carrots into chunks and have the students join them with toothpicks to form carrot sculptures.

2. Cut off the carrot tops and put them in water to grow carrot "ferns."

3. Create a carrot patch by sequencing all the carrots shortest to longest.

4. Measure the carrots as a group. Then prepare and eat them for a healthy snack.

Books to Read Aloud: Basic Concepts of Measurement by Brian D. Ellis; Measuring by Richard Allington; Little, Too Tall by Jane B. Moncure; Big and Small, Short and Tall by Ron Ray.

Carrot Patterns

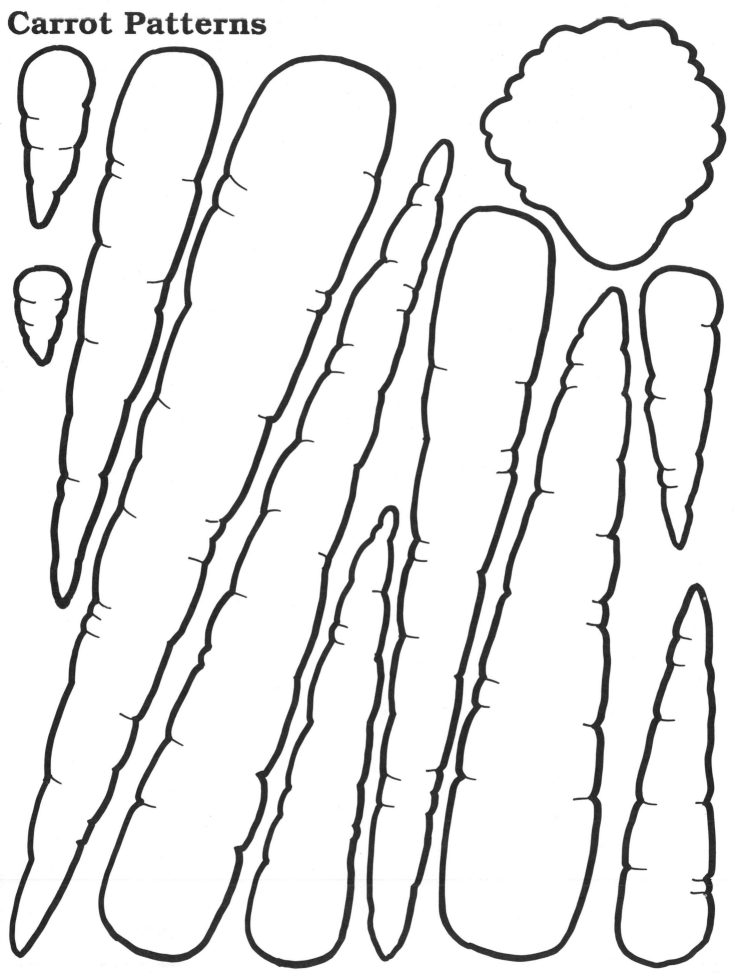

Name _____

Write the length of each of the carrots you measured on the bulletin board.

Charlie's Measuring

1. _____

2. _____

3. _____

4. _____

5. _____

6. _____

7. _____

8. _____

9. _____

10. _____

Name _____

Help Charlie measure these carrots in centimeters.

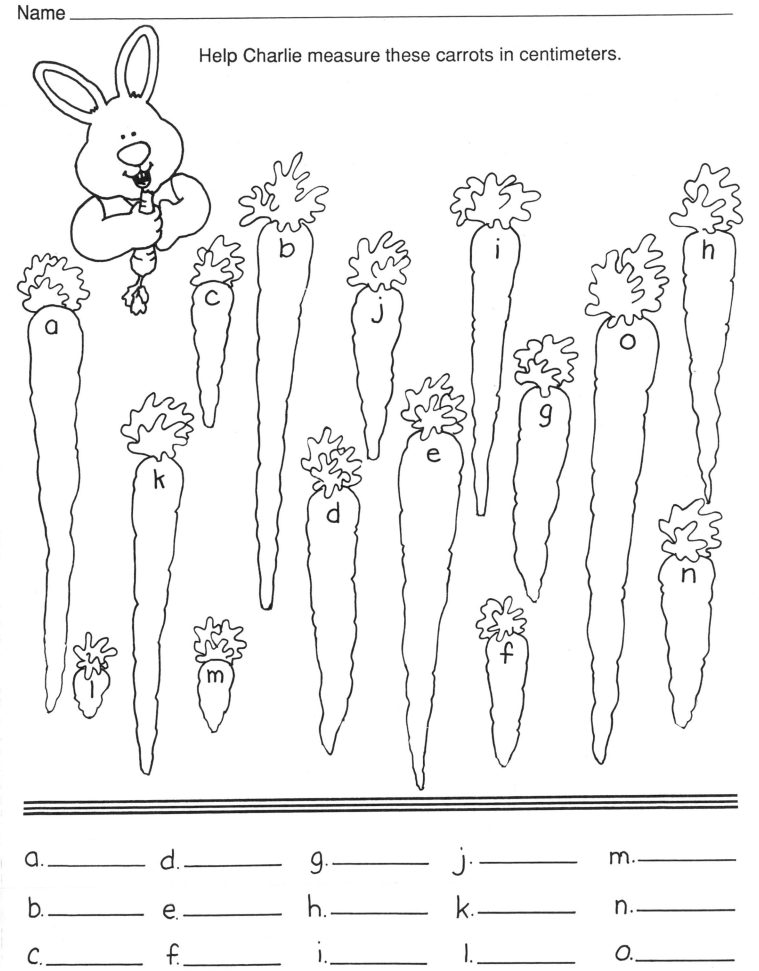

a. _____   d. _____   g. _____   j. _____   m. _____

b. _____   e. _____   h. _____   k. _____   n. _____

c. _____   f. _____   i. _____   l. _____   o. _____

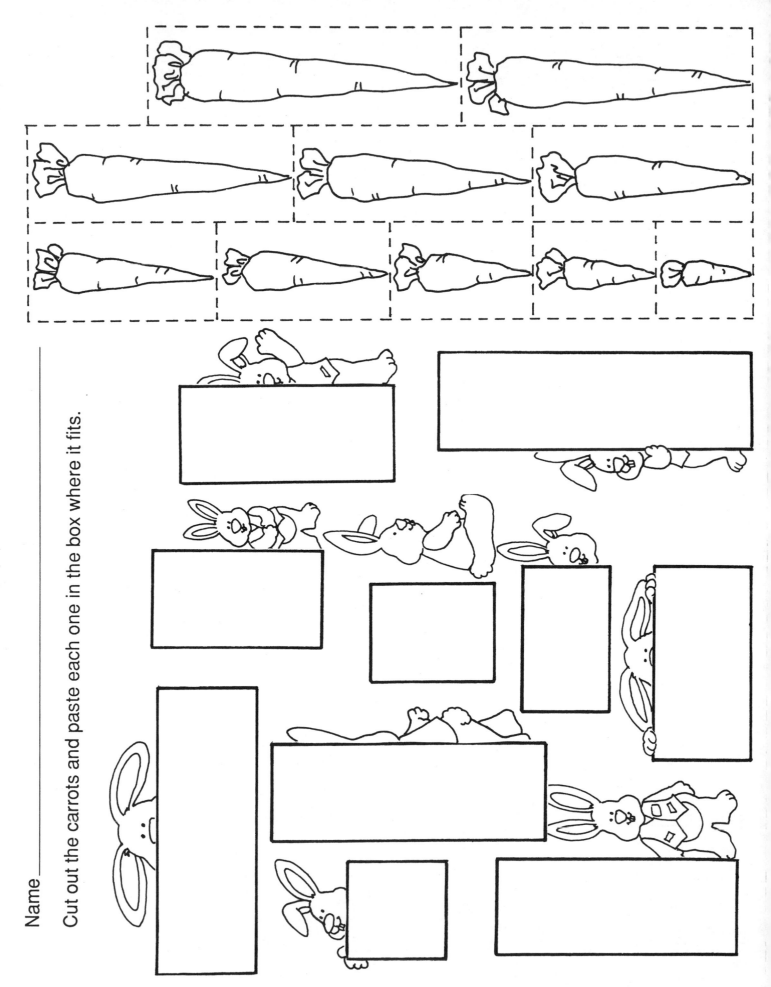

Name _____

Cut out the carrots and paste each one in the box where it fits.

_____'s **Homework**

Dear Parents,

    We are working on measuring skills. Please purchase some carrots and help your child measure them to determine the longest and shortest carrot in the group. Fill in the answers below, rounding to the nearest inch or centimeter. Then complete the rest of the page. Have your child bring this paper and the two carrots to class for a group activity.

My shortest carrot is _____ long.

My longest carrot is _____ long.

List the people in your family who like carrots: _____

_____

_____

List the people in your family who do not like carrots: _____

_____

_____

Activity 3: Find My Ear

Objective: To be able to match uppercase and lowercase letters

Materials: Patterns, scissors, pink and other colors of construction paper, felt-tip pen, stencils (optional), stapler, plastic bag, pushpins

Construction: Enlarge and duplicate the Charlie pattern from pink construction paper and mount it on the board. Duplicate and cut out 26 rabbit head patterns and 26 ear patterns. Stencil or write one uppercase letter on each ear on the rabbit head pattern and a lowercase letter on each unattached ear pattern. Staple the rabbit head patterns to the board, placing two staples on the head for an ear pattern to slip into. Laminate the ear patterns and store them in a plastic bag pinned to the board. Decorate the board and put up the title "Find My Ear."

Directions: Review with the children the letters of the alphabet in their uppercase and lowercase forms. Then tell the students they will be completing pictures of Charlie by adding missing ears. Show them how to match a lowercase letter on an ear pattern to its uppercase form on the rabbit pattern by sliding the ear pattern between the staples on the head. Check the students' work when completed.

Variation: Write the first part of a compound word on an ear attached to a rabbit head pattern; write the last part of the compound word on a separate ear. Have the students match ear patterns to rabbit head patterns to form compound words.

Worksheet: Write a capital letter in each left side of each bow tie before you duplicate the worksheet. Have the students fill in the lowercase letters on the right sides. For younger children, put sets of dots on the left side of the bows and have the students write the corresponding numeral on the right side.

Parent Letter: You may want to change the letters to be colored to suit the letters you have been working on in class. The alphabet letters could also be rearranged so that they form a picture when the correct letters are colored.

Books to Read Aloud: Dr. Seuss's ABC by Dr. Seuss; I Spy ABC by Pam Adams; Letters by Richard Allington.

Rabbit and Ear Patterns

Name

29

Dear Parents,

For this activity your child will need red, yellow, and green crayons. The object is to locate and color all uppercase and lowercase B's with the red crayon; all uppercase and lowercase D's with the yellow crayon; and all uppercase and lowercase P's with the green crayon. The other letters do not get colored. Have your child return the paper to school.

M	P	L	d	t	G	D	I	b	A
T	X	U	Y	P	L	R	Q	C	S
S	D	x	B	n	W	P	T	D	Z
u	b	m	i	d	q	k	d	h	v
w	g	f	s	c	B	A	l	P	a
G	O	B	E	D	S	H	P	F	z
f	P	V	P	b	a	d	r	J	d
M	t	e	u	N	P	Y	B	o	C
V	F	B	X	E	Y	K	R	H	b
P	L	e	P	Z	b	h	c	D	a

Activity 4: Where's Charlie?

Objective: To recognize Charlie in ordinal positions, first through tenth

Materials: Patterns, scissors, construction paper, pink crayon, plastic bag, stapler, pushpins, paste or glue stick, felt-tip pen

Construction: Duplicate and cut out 10 each of the Charlie and friend strip patterns. Glue two strips together to form 10 longer strips. Color one rabbit pink (Charlie) in a different ordinal position in each of the 10 strips. Mount the strips on the bulletin board. Place a pin next to each strip. Then make 10 ordinal labels: first, second, third, and so on. Laminate the labels and store them in a plastic bag hung on the board. Decorate the bulletin board and put up the title "Where's Charlie?"

Directions: Review the ordinal position words first through tenth with the students. Then remind them that Charlie is a pink rabbit. Tell them that Charlie is lost, and they must find him on each strip of rabbits on the board. Tell them to locate each Charlie by hanging the correct ordinal word that tells where Charlie is. For example, if Charlie is the third rabbit in a strip, they should hang the label "Third" under that Charlie. Practice hanging up labels with the children. Then have them complete the exercise. Check the students' work.

Variations:

• For kindergarten students, you may want to shorten the rabbit strips and always color Charlie in either first or last position. Have the children hang labels that say "First" or "Last," or just "F" or "L," under each Charlie.

• Change the variation above by using strips showing a variety of animals.

• Hold up each Charlie and Friend strip and have the children write the correct ordinal word for Charlie's position on a paper numbered 1 to 10.

Worksheets: You may vary the first worksheet by changing it to a review of number sequence. Delete the ordinal word at the beginning of each line and then number each shape in order, leaving one shape blank. Have the children fill in the missing numbers.

Charlie and Friend Strip Patterns

Name _____

Read each word and color the right shape.

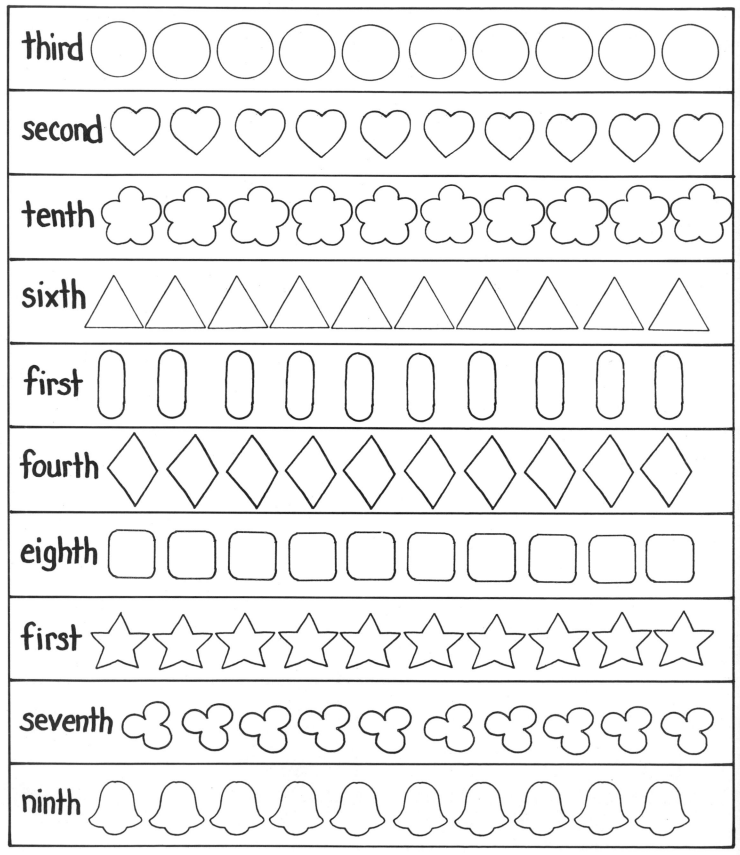

third
second
tenth
sixth
first
fourth
eighth
first
seventh
ninth

Name _____

Which rabbit's vest has been colored in? Write F for first or L for last.

Dear Parents,

This is a family activity, so please try to involve your whole family in it. Start by discussing who is the oldest, or was born first, in your family. Write that name on the first rung of the ladder. Continue placing family members' names on the ladder in the order in which the people were born. If your immediate family is small, include other relatives.

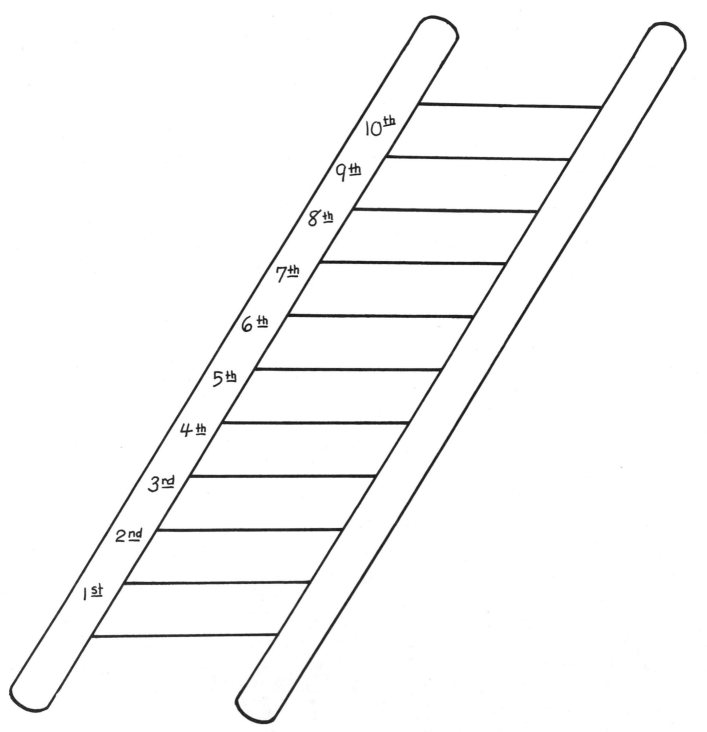

© 1990 Monday Morning Books, Inc.

This is Baxter. Baxter is a red-headed boy who is very adventurous. The skills Baxter teaches through his bulletin board activities are:

1. Size sequencing

2. Safety

3. Recognizing beginning sounds

4. Matching beginning sounds

Baxter Pattern

Baxter

Baxter's Bubbles

Activity 1: Baxter's Bubbles

Objective: To be able to sequence a set of bubbles according to size

Materials: Patterns, scissors, eight colors of construction paper, hole punch, plastic bags, stapler, pushpins

Construction: Enlarge and cut out a Baxter pattern and mount it on the board. Then use the bubble patterns to make as many sets of bubbles and as many bubbles in each set as you want; cut each set out of a different color of construction paper. Punch a hole in the top of each bubble pattern and laminate all of them. Place each set in a plastic bag hung on the board. Place as many pins on the board as there are bubbles in a set. Decorate the board and put up the title "Baxter's Bubbles."

Directions: Review the concept of big and little. Then introduce the activity by distributing bubbles and wands and letting the children blow bubbles. Tell the students that Baxter's bubbles start out small and get bigger and bigger. Spread a set of paper bubbles on the floor and show the class how to sequence them according to size. Then demonstrate how to hang the bubble patterns in a row on the board from smallest to biggest. Check the children's work after they've hung up all the bubbles. Have the children try again if any bubbles are out of sequence.

Variation: Change the activity to "Baxter's String of Fish." Instead of bubble patterns, have the children sequence fish patterns that are the same size but display a different number. Direct the children to hang the fish in a row from the fish with the smallest number to the one with the biggest number.

Worksheet: Extend the practice of size sequencing by having the children cut and paste different-sized fish, from smallest to biggest.

Books to Read Aloud: Very Last Time First by Jan Andrews; Size: The Measure of Things by Eric Laithwate; Who Is Next? by Grahame Corbett; Learn About Color and Shape and Size by Diana Courson; Sizes by Gillian Youldon.

Bubble Patterns

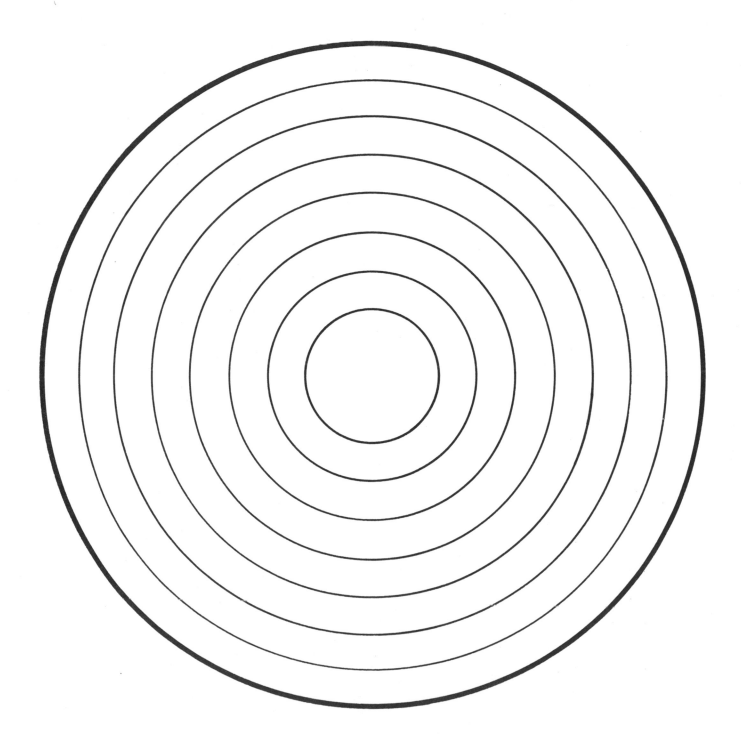

Name _____

Cut out each fish and paste it in a box in order from smallest to largest.

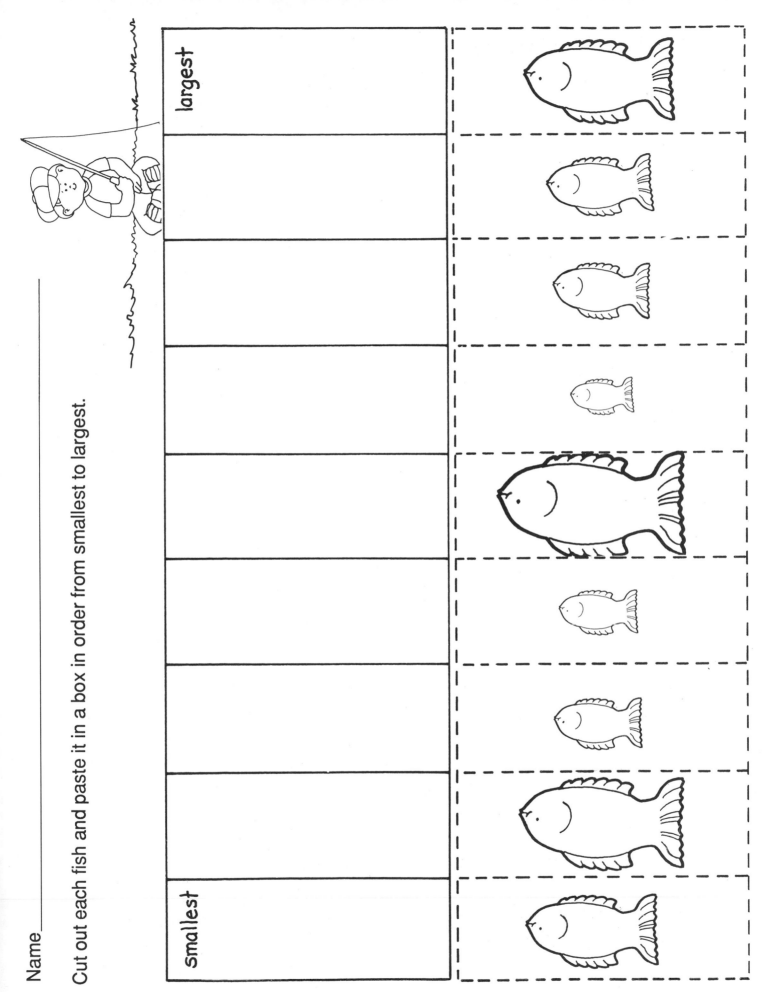

largest

smallest

Dear Parents,

   Please collect as many different sizes of nails or bolts as you can find.   Then help your child sequence them from smallest to largest and tape them in order on this paper. Mount the paper on a sturdy piece of cardboard. Have your child return the collection to class.

My Nail Collection

Baxter Practices Sign Safety

Activity 2:
Baxter Practices Sign Safety

Objective: To understand the meanings of signs used for safety and information in everyday life

Materials: Patterns, scissors, construction paper, tagboard, hole punch, crayons, felt-tip pen, pushpins, plastic bag, stapler

Construction: Enlarge and duplicate the Baxter pattern and mount it on the board. Enlarge and duplicate the sign patterns you want to use and color them in appropriately. Then, on strips of tagboard, write a few words that tell about each sign. For instance, for the stop sign you might write "Do not go"; for the sign that shows a person in a crosswalk you might write "People walking." Punch a hole in each end of each tagboard strip and laminate all the strips. Then mount the street signs on the board and store the tagboard strips in a bag hung on the board. Place pins on the board for hanging. Decorate the board and mount the title "Baxter Practices Sign Safety."

Directions: Discuss with the class how signs are important to safety and how signs provide a lot of information about the world around us. Call on students to choose a sign on the bulletin board and tell in their own words what it means. Then tell the class that Baxter has just learned to ride a bike. Before he goes riding, he needs help learning about safety signs. Ask the students to help him by going to the board and choosing a tagboard strip. Then read the strip to the children. Have them hang it under the appropriate safety sign. Check the students' work. After the activity, you may want to have the students draw a safety poster that shows some of the signs that have been discussed.

Variations:

- Mount containers or pictures of containers of different breakfast foods, such as cereal, bread, doughnuts, juice, and so on. Have the children hang a happy face, which indicates good nutrition, or a sad face, which indicates poor nutrition, under each item.

- Discuss school safety rules and then let each child select a rule he or she would like to illustrate. Have the children make their drawings into safety posters. Write a short phrase about each safety rule on each poster.

Worksheets: The first worksheet may be used as a test at the end of the activity. The second worksheet also reviews safety.

Books to Read Aloud: Let's Stay Safe & Sound by The Bank Street College of Education Staff; Strangers Don't Look Like The Big Bad Wolf! by Janis Buchman and Debbie Hunley; I Read Signs by Tana Hoban; When I Cross The Street by Dorothy Chlad.

Sign Patterns

YIELD

DO NOT
ENTER

ENTRANCE

To the teacher: Read the following sentences to the children. Direct them to color a happy face if the sentence tells them something safe to do. Have them color a sad face if the sentence tells them something unsafe to do.

1. Don't bother wearing a seat belt.
2. Walk facing the traffic.
3. Stop signs are only for cars.
4. Chase your ball into the street.
5. If you find pills, eat them.

6. If you get lost, stay where you are.
7. Never accept candy from a stranger.
8. House plants can be poisonous.
9. Look both ways before you cross the street.
10. Matches are fun to play with.

Name

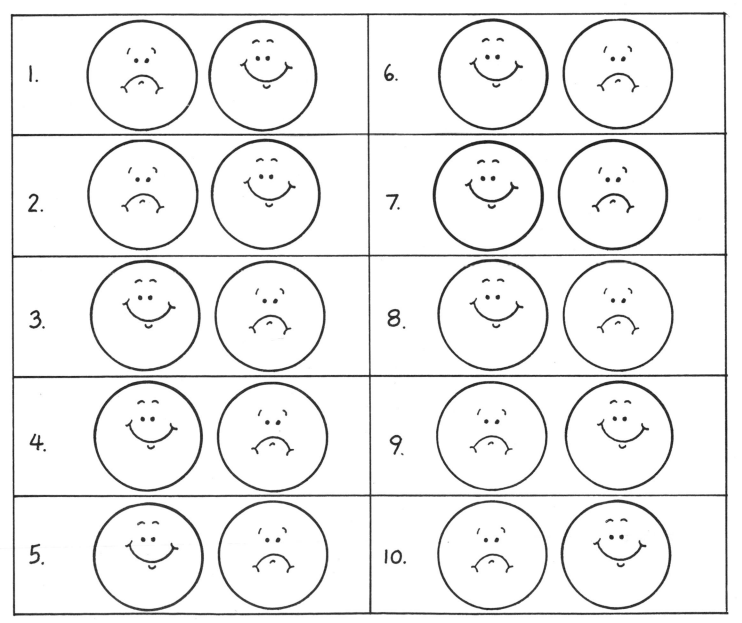

Name _____

Draw a line between safety signs that match.

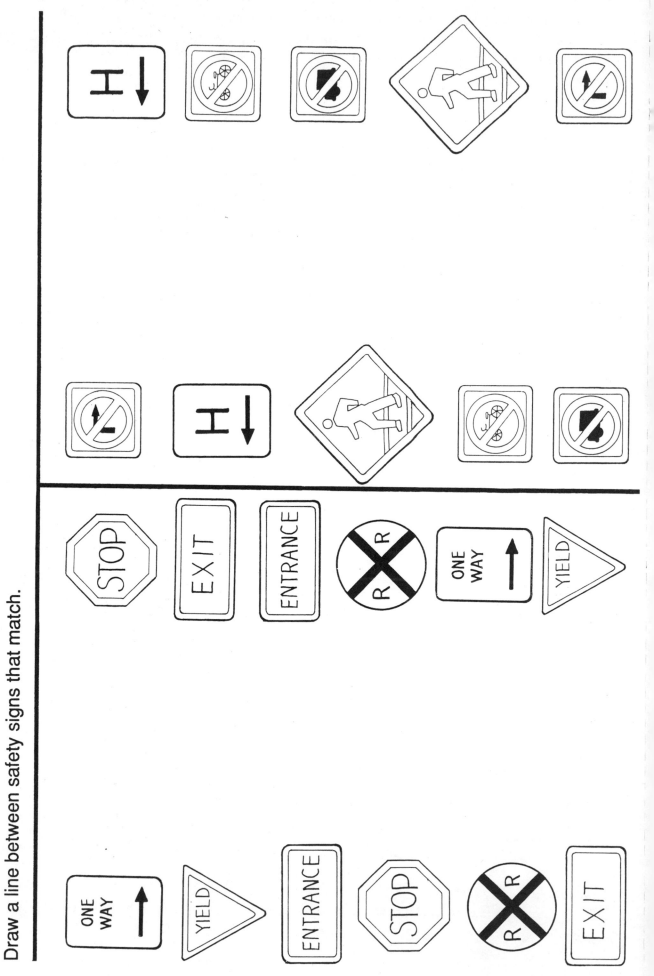

_____'s Homework

Dear Parents,

    This activity can benefit your whole family. Complete the lower section of this paper together by finding out the appropriate telephone numbers and writing them on the chart. Post the numbers in a convenient place by the telephone. Discuss with your child why he or she might need the numbers. If your child does not know how to use the telephone, practice the skill now. Ask family members to help you act out possible emergency situations.

Emergency Numbers

Fire
Department
_____

Poison
Control
_____

Ambulance
_____

Neighbor or
Relative
_____

Police
_____

Doctor
_____

Baxter's Brown Bags

Activity 3: Baxter's Brown Bags

Objective: To match alphabet letters with pictures of beginning consonant sounds

Materials: Pattern, scissors, old magazines or other reading materials, glue, index cards (optional), construction paper, brown lunch bags, felt-tip pen or stencils, X-acto knife, stapler, plastic bag, pushpins

Construction: Enlarge and duplicate the Baxter pattern and mount it on the board. Decide which consonant sounds you would like to work with on this activity. Cut out from old magazines small pictures of objects that begin with the sound of each of the letters you will work with (make multiple sets for learning station groups). Glue the pictures to index cards or construction paper cards. Roll down the tops of as many lunch bags as you need and write, stencil, or glue a consonant on one side of each. Laminate the picture cards and the bags. Then split open the top of each bag with the knife. Staple the bags to the bulletin board and store the cards in a plastic bag hung on the board. Decorate the bulletin board and mount the title "Baxter's Brown Bags."

Directions: Be sure the children can recognize consonant letters and their sounds. Then review the letters that are on the lunch bags as well as the sounds they make. Tell the class that they will be helping Baxter sort picture cards into lunch bags. Demonstrate how to drop a card into the bag labeled with the beginning letter of the picture. Have the children put all the cards into the correct bags. Check their work, and have them redo any cards that are in the wrong bags.

Variations:

- Mount four lunch bags, each of which is labeled with one of the four food groups. Have the students categorize cards showing pictures of food by dropping each card into the correct bag.

- Let more advanced students drop word cards into the appropriate beginning consonant bags. Then have them write the words on a piece of paper in alphabetical order.

Worksheets: In the first worksheet, children cut and paste pictures that begin with the designated letter. In the second, they cut and paste pictures that end with the letter.

Books to Read Aloud: The Little Golden ABC by Cornelius De Witt; Silly Alphabet Letters by Ann Hardy.

Name

Match the picture on the ball that begins with the letter on the bat.
Cut out the picture and paste it in the space below the bat.

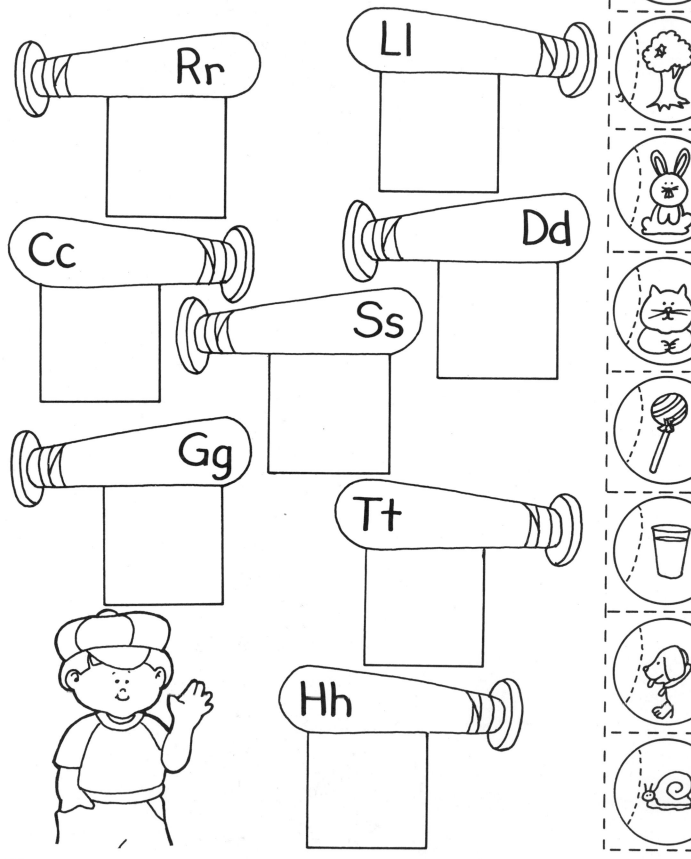

Name_____

Match the picture in the wheel that ends with the letter on the car.
Cut out the picture and paste it in the wheel on the car.

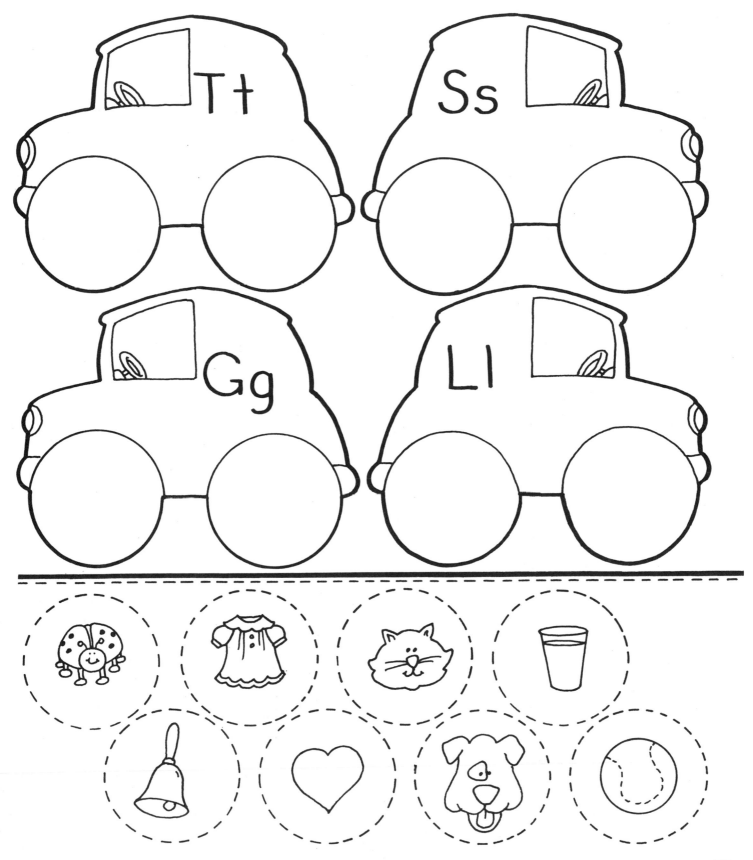

_____'s **Homework**

Dear Parents,

   Your child needs to be able to hear the beginning sound of a word and correctly identify objects that begin with the same sound. Please find attached a small brown bag that your child should fill with three or more objects that begin with the letter sound on the front of the bag. For example, if the letter on the bag is a Y, your child might put a yo-yo, a piece of yarn, and something yellow in the bag. When the bag has been filled, help your child fill out the form below. Please send both the form and the bag back to school with your child. We will open the bag there and look at all the things that were found. As we learn new letters, please repeat the activity at home for reinforcement.

_____   _____
            name   date

                        _____
                        teacher signature

I returned my brown bag
with _____ objects.

I have learned the
beginning sound _____.

Baxter's Bike

Activity 4: Baxter's Bike

Objective: To match two pictures that begin with the same sound

Materials: Patterns, scissors, construction paper, heavy-weight paper, brads, felt-tip pen, stapler, pushpins

Construction: Enlarge and duplicate the Baxter pattern and mount it on the bulletin board. Enlarge and duplicate the bicycle pattern. Cut out the area inside the dotted lines on the bicycle, then laminate the bicycle so a window forms in the empty space. Make a copy of each filled-in wheel pattern from heavy paper. Fill in the empty wheel with pictures from your reading series and duplicate and cut out two of these wheels from heavy paper. Choose the two wheels you'd like to use first and attach one with a brad to the back of each bicycle wheel. Mount the bicycle on the board so the wheels can turn freely. Be sure each picture can be seen through each wheel's "window." Decorate the bulletin board and mount the title "Baxter's Bike."

Directions: Be sure the students have some understanding of how to listen for sounds that are the same. Then let the students relate any experiences they have had riding a bicycle. Discuss bicycle safety. Then tell the children that they can help Baxter fix his bicycle wheels by matching pictures with the same beginning sound. Turn one wheel to show a picture with a particular beginning sound. Ask the first student to turn the other wheel to find another picture that begins with the same sound. Continue the activity until all the children have turned the wheel. Substitute the second set of wheels for additional practice. Let two students work together without you after they are familiar with the activity.

Worksheet: Read each set of words to the children. Have them color the happy face if the words have the same beginning sound and color the sad face if the words have different beginning sounds. Extend the activity by preparing and reading pairs of words with the same and different middle sounds and ending sounds. Pairs of rhyming and non-rhyming words can also be used.

Parent Letter: Before you duplicate and distribute this assignment, write one of the letters you want to work on in each of the boxes provided. Draw or paste a picture in each of the pie wedges of something that begins with each of the letter sounds.

Books to Read Aloud: My "B" Sound Box by Jane B. Moncure; Cowboy Alphabet by James Right; Bicycles Are Fun to Ride by Dorothy Chlad; My First Bike by Donald Keefe; The Bike Lesson by Stan and Jan Berenstain.

Bicycle Pattern

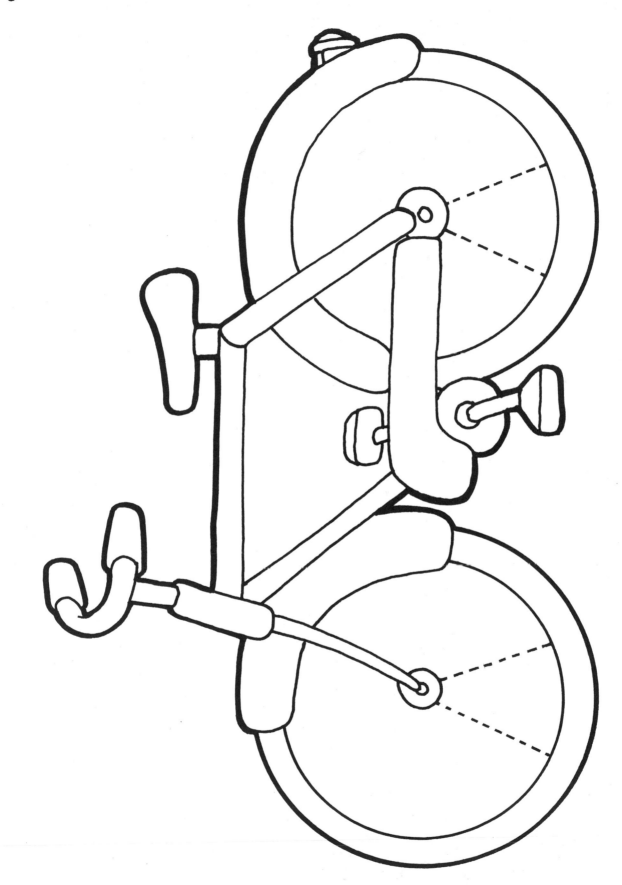

Wheel Patterns

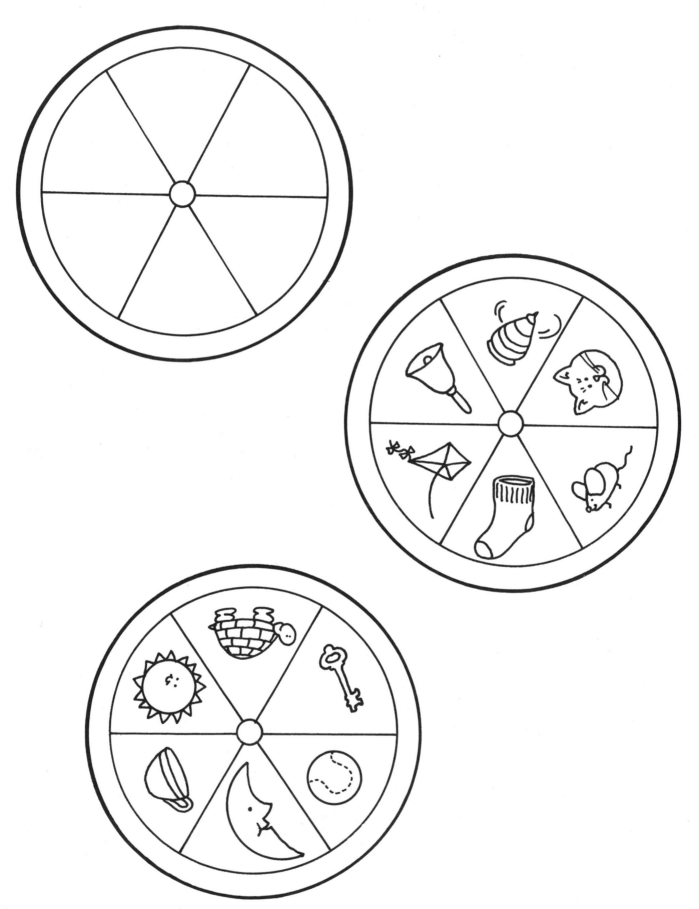

Name

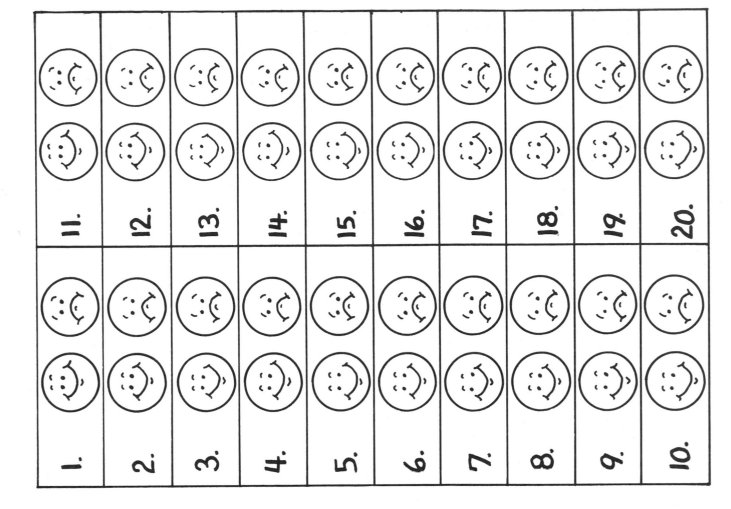

To the teacher: Read each pair of words to the students. Then direct them to color the happy face if the words begin with the same sound. Have them color the sad face if the words are different.

Word List

1. apple, saddle
2. boot, box
3. vest, view
4. cup, mug
5. foot, loot
6. rug, road
7. trail, tail
8. happy, silly
9. drop, drain
10. yellow, yawn

11. market, morning
12. last, clasp
13. hard, choose
14. sugar, sand
15. green, flea
16. queen, quilt
17. work, wood
18. nine, wasp
19. born, rain
20. seat, ball

Dear Parents,

    Cut out the picture in each pie-shaped wedge and have your child say the beginning sound. Ask your child to match the picture's beginning sound to one of the letters in a box above the bicycle wheels. Help your child glue the correct four pictures onto each bicycle wheel. Have your child return the paper to class.

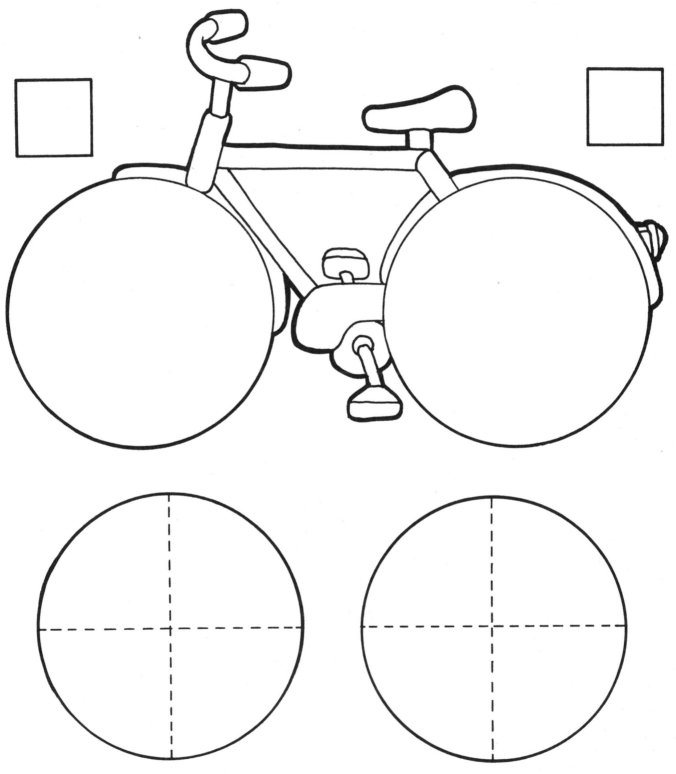

This is Penny. Penny always wears overalls, and lives on a farm with chickens, pigs, and a potato patch. The skills Penny teaches through her bulletin board activities are:

1. Alphabetical order
2. Spelling own name
3. Number sets 1 to 10
4. Classification

Penny Pattern

Penny

65

Penny Hangs the Wash

Activity 1: Penny Hangs the Wash

Objective: To sequence letters of the alphabet in correct order

Materials: Patterns, scissors, stapler, construction paper, heavy cord or light rope, stencils, felt-tip pen, or glue, clothespins, mini-laundry basket, small container

Construction: Enlarge and duplicate the Penny pattern and mount it on the bulletin board. Enlarge and duplicate the laundry patterns and cut them out. On each laundry pattern, stencil, write, or glue on a different alphabet letter. Use capital letters for kindergarten students, lowercase letters for first graders. Be sure the letters are placed on the patterns in the upright position for easy reading. Laminate the patterns and store them in the laundry basket near the board. Put the clothespins in a small container. Staple several lengths of cord or rope to the board for the children to hang the laundry patterns on. Decorate the bulletin board and mount the title "Penny Hangs the Wash."

Directions: Be sure the children are able to say the alphabet with a fair degree of accuracy. Then initiate a discussion about laundry day. Have the children tell how their parents dry the clothes. Some will mention dryers, others will talk about clotheslines. Then introduce Penny and tell the students that it's her day to do the laundry. Explain to the children that they will help Penny hang the wash by arranging all the clothes in alphabetical order. Discuss the items that are in the laundry basket. Then lay the laundry patterns on the floor or a table with each pattern's letter showing. Have the students hang the laundry patterns on the clothesline in alphabetical order, working individually or in pairs. Check their work when completed.

Variations:

- Let the children wear clothespin aprons while doing the activity. Both the clothespins and the laundry patterns can be kept in the apron pockets as the children work.

- Write a word on each laundry pattern and let older children hang the patterns in alphabetical order by word.

- Put a numeral on each laundry pattern and have the students hang the patterns in numerical order.

Worksheet: The worksheet is designed for students to fill in capital letters at the top and lowercase letters at the bottom.

Books to Read Aloud: Alfred's Alphabet Walk by Victoria Chess; Hosie's Alphabet by Leonard Baskin; Indian Two Feet and the ABC Moose Hunt by Margaret Friskey; ABC-an Alphabet Book by Thomas Natthiesen.

Laundry Patterns

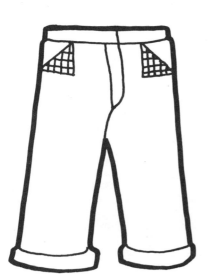

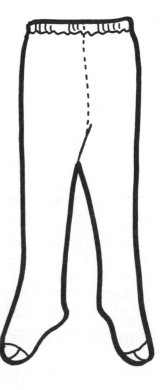

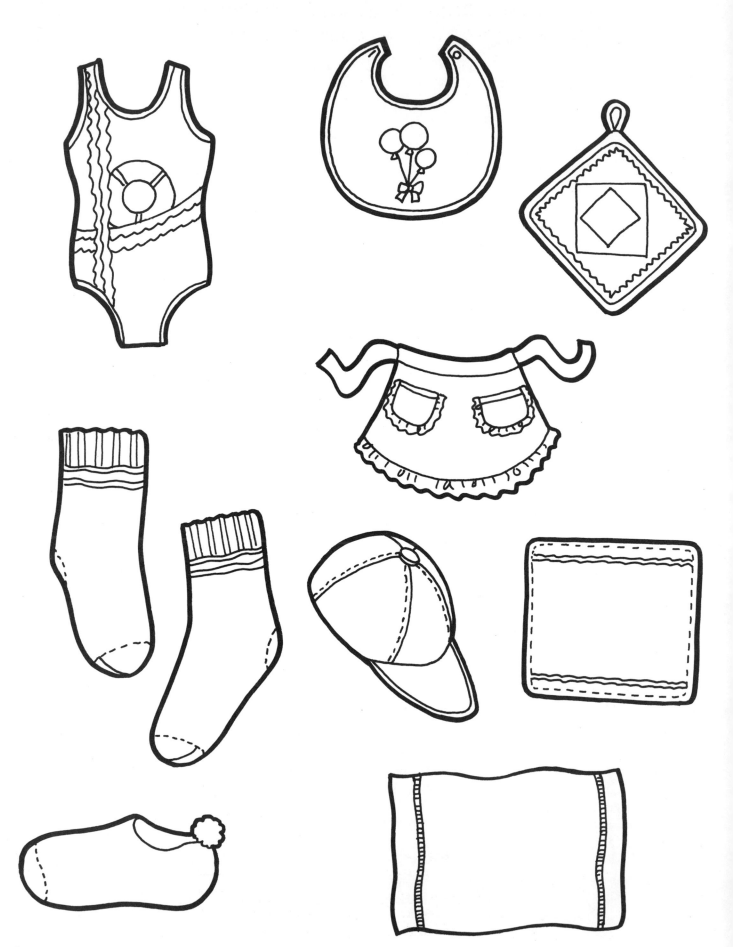

Name _____

Fill in the missing capital letters of the alphabet in the first caterpillar.
Fill in the missing lowercase letters in the second caterpillar.

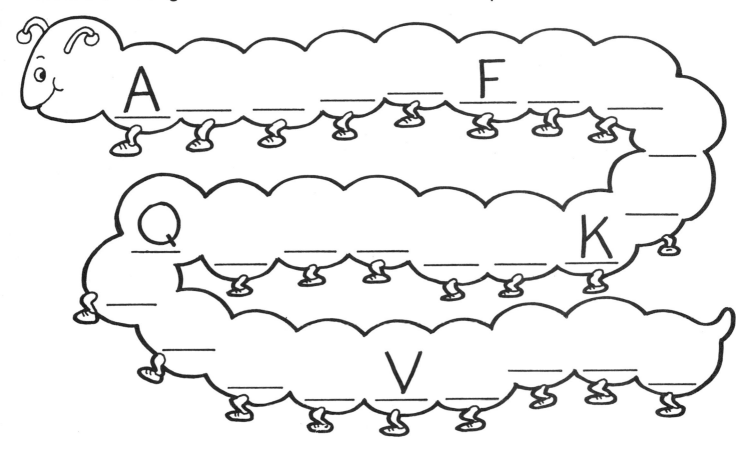

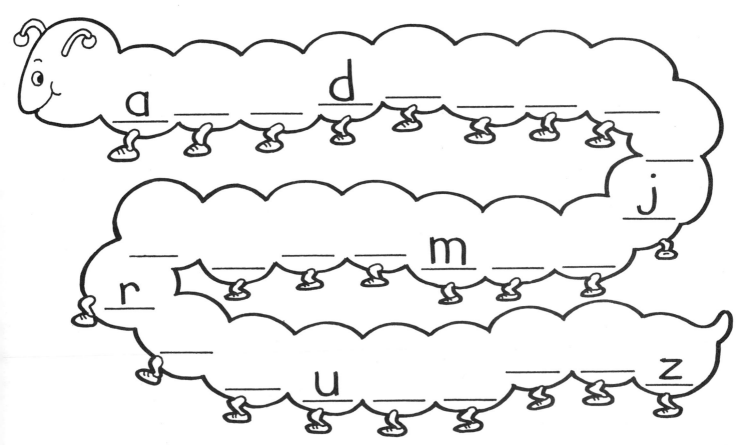

Dear Parents,

We have been learning how to write the letters of the alphabet. Please help your child write the lowercase alphabet letters on the beach towel below. Then cut out the beach towel and let your child decorate it on the back. Have your child bring the work back to school tomorrow.

a b c d e f g h i j k l m
n o p q r s t u v w x y z

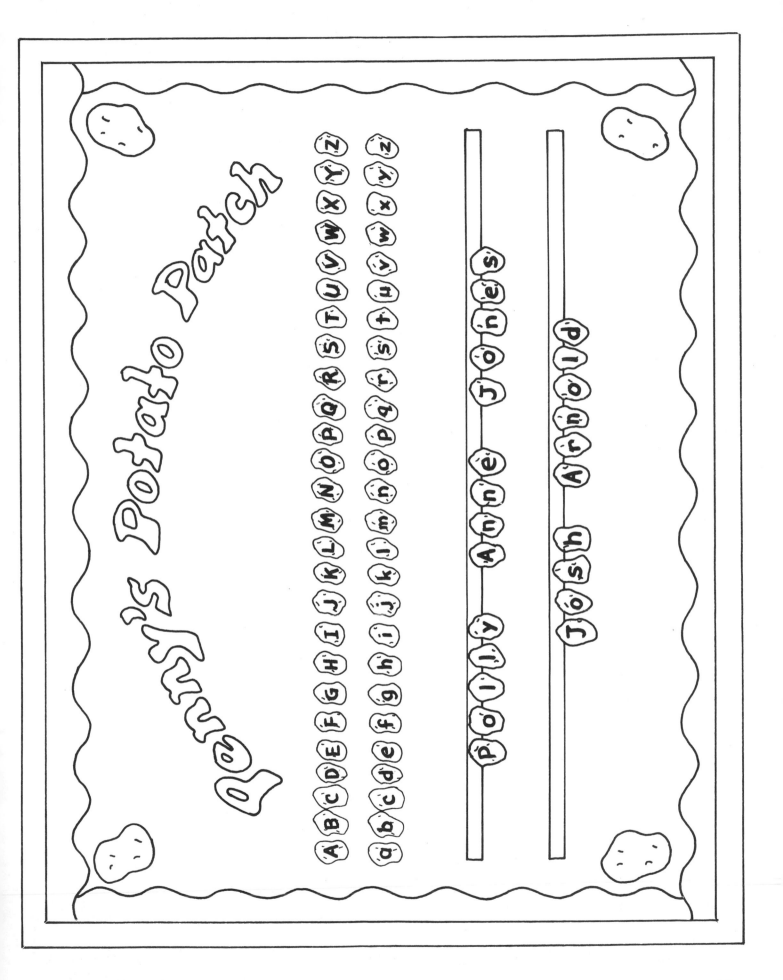

Penny's Potato Patch

A B C D E F G H I J K L M N O P Q R S T U V W X Y Z

a b c d e f g h i j k l m n o p q r s t u v w x y z

Polly Anne Jones

Josh Arnold

Activity 2: Penny's Potato Patch

Objective: To have the children select the letters in their name and be able to arrange them in order

Materials: Patterns, scissors, light-brown and another color of construction paper, Velcro circles and strips, stapler or pushpins

Construction: Duplicate and cut out from light-brown construction paper one set of capital letter potato patterns and three sets of lowercase letter potato patterns. Review your children's names to see if there are any additional letters you will need to make. Laminate the potato patterns. Attach a Velcro circle to the back of each pattern. Then place two long Velcro strips, one above the other, about halfway up the board. Press the potato patterns with capital letters—in alphabetical order—on the top row of Velcro; press the lowercase letters in order on the lower strip. Next, place a shorter Velcro strip near the bottom of the board (put up several strips if more than one student will work at at time). Decorate the board and add the title "Penny's Potato Patch."

Directions: Discuss the letters of the alphabet with the children. Then tell them they will be showing Penny how to spell their names with the potatoes in her patch. Show the students how to take down potato patterns and press them onto the lower Velcro strip. Then have them take turns choosing the letters in their names and putting them in order on the strip. Check their work. At the end of the activity, have the children return the letters to the proper places on the upper rows of Velcro.

Variations:

- Make 20 potato cutouts (two blank potato patterns are provided) and stencil a number word from one to twenty on each. Have the children press the patterns on a strip of Velcro in numerical word order.

- Use the letters on the potato patterns to have the children practice forming simple sight words.

Award: Congratulate the children with the award that follows when they have mastered writing their names. Have them write their best effort on the line in the middle of the award.

Books to Read Aloud: We Laughed A Lot My First Day of School by Sylvia Root Tester; First, Middle, and Nick: All About Names by Barbara S. Hazen; Names and Their Meanings by Leopold Wagner; David's Book by Anne Rothman and Kenneth Hicks; I'm Terrific by Margorie Weiman Sharmat.

Potato Patterns

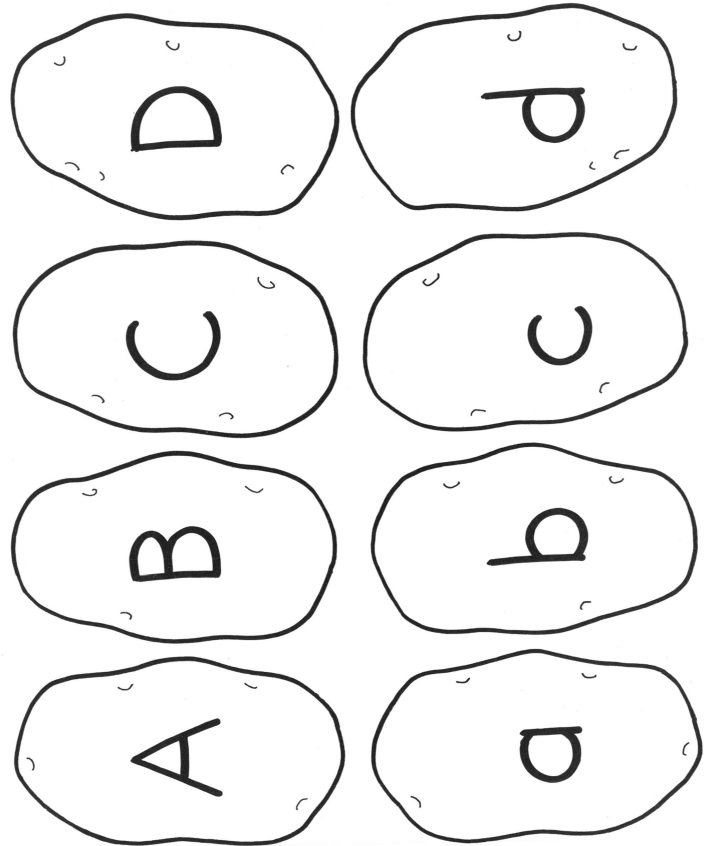

75

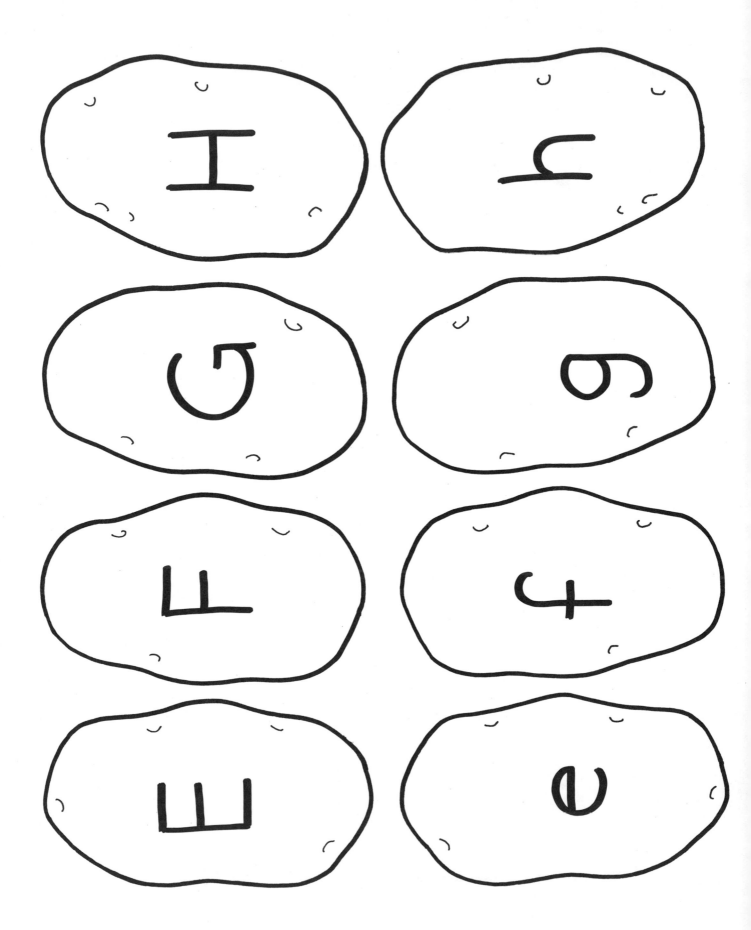

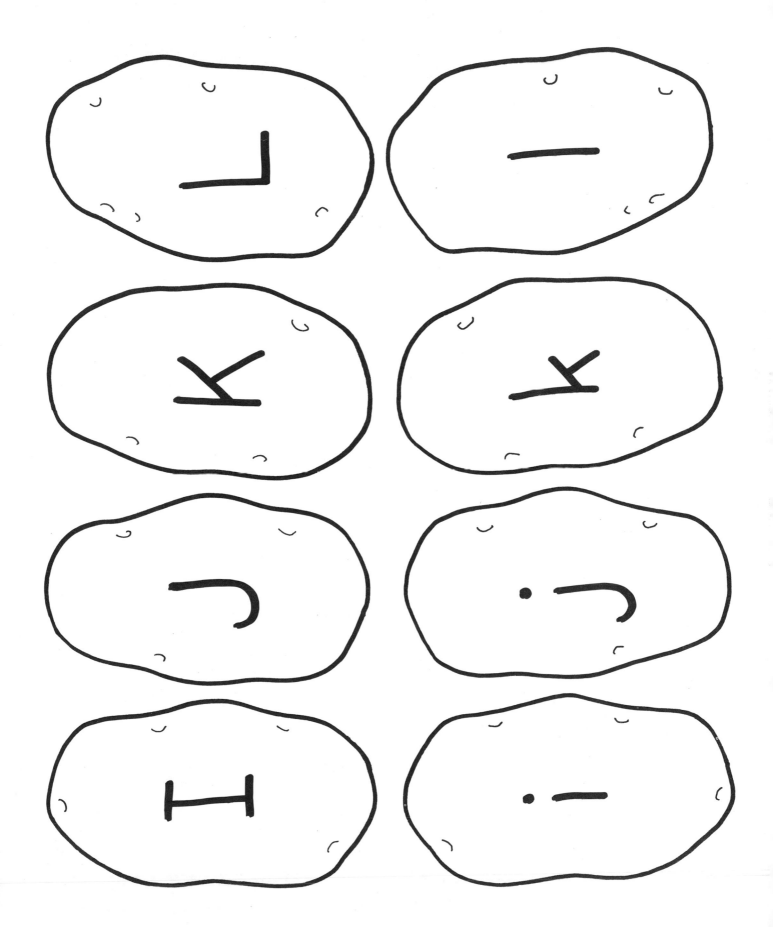

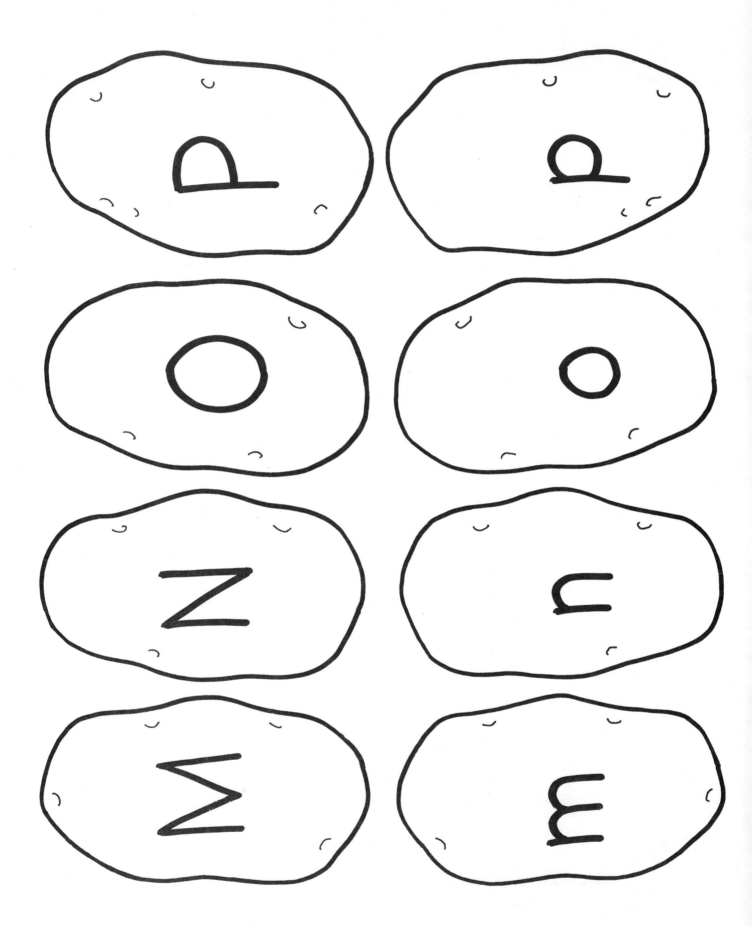

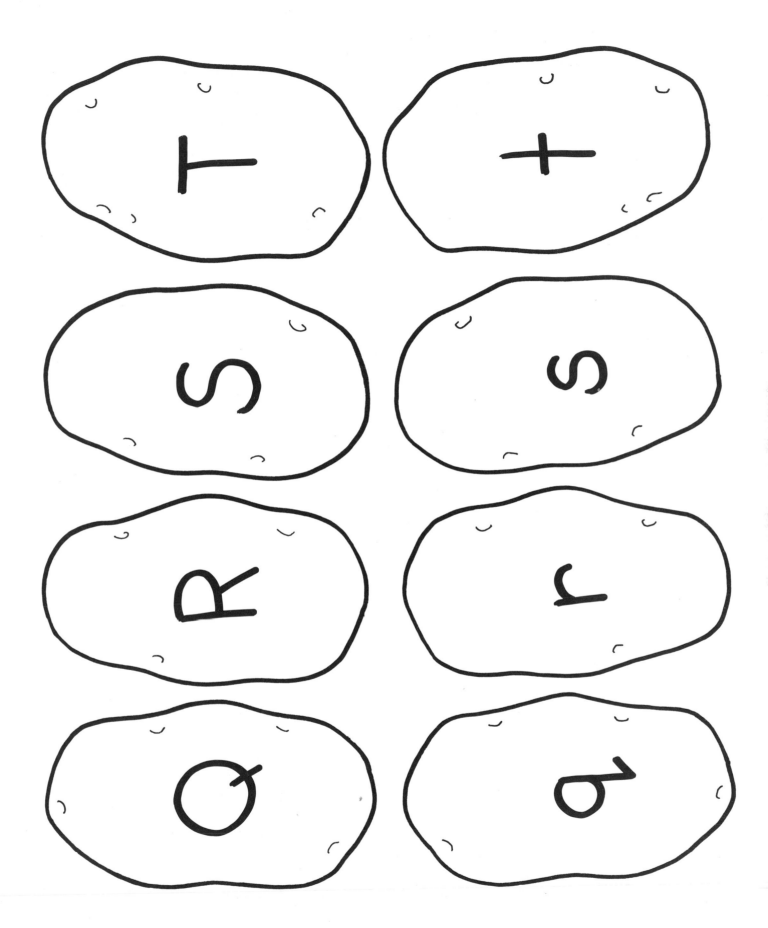

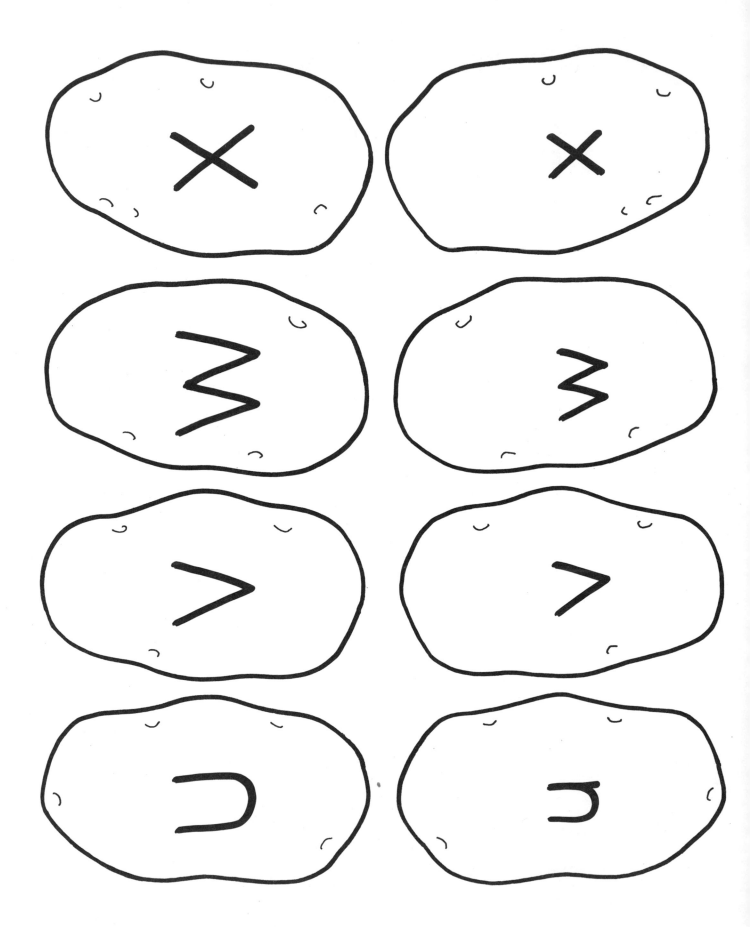

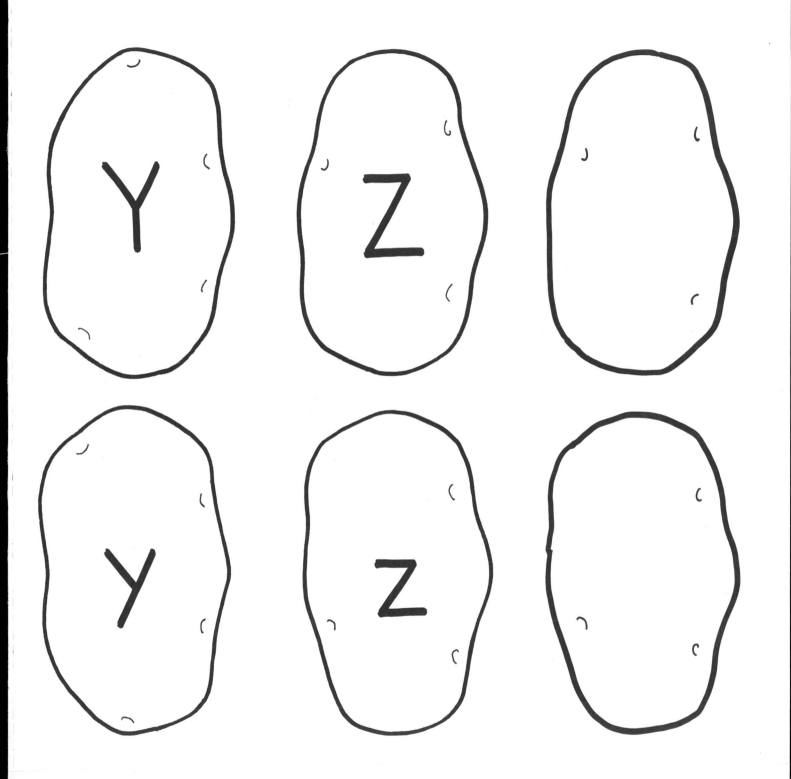

Penny is proud
of _____
for writing his name.

signed _____

Penny is proud
of _____
for writing her name.

signed _____

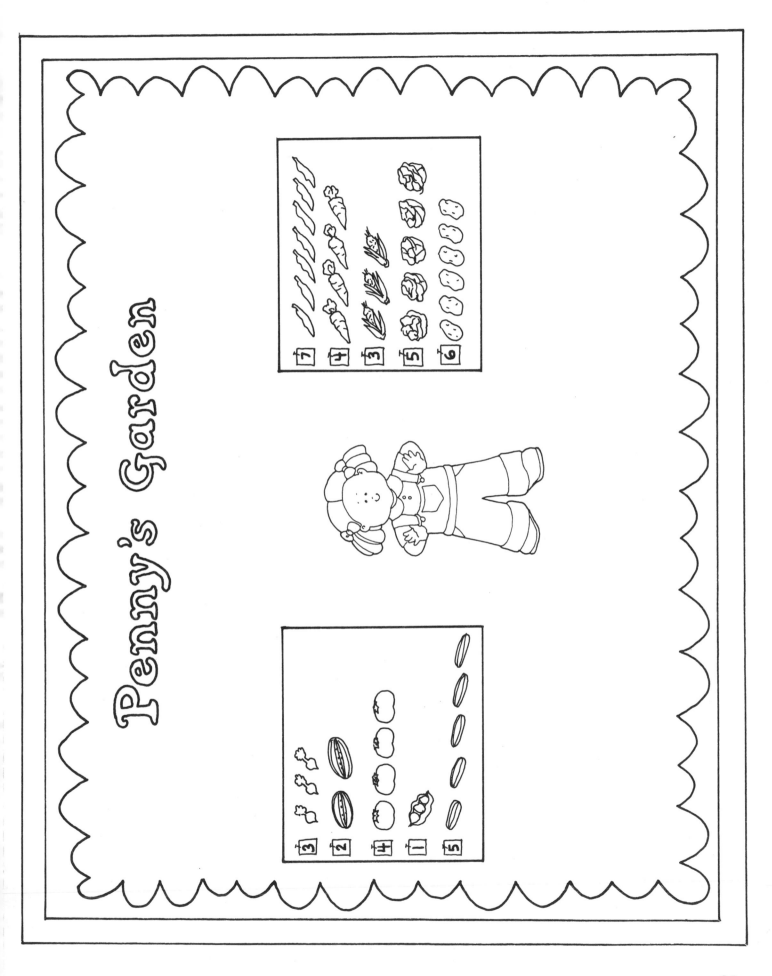

Penny's Garden

Activity 3: Penny's Garden

Objective: To count sets of objects from 1 to 10

Materials: Patterns, scissors, green, red, brown, orange, light-brown, and yellow construction paper, index cards, stapler, pushpins, plastic bag, stencils, felt-tip pen, hole punch

Construction: Enlarge and duplicate a Penny pattern and mount it on the bulletin board. Duplicate and cut out the various vegetable patterns in sets ranging from 1 to 10. Use yellow construction paper for the corn cutouts, red for the radish cutouts, and so on; make the garden area from light-brown construction paper. Mount a row of each type of vegetable in the garden. Put a pin at the beginning of each row. Then stencil a numeral from 1 to 10 on the index cards. Laminate the cards and punch a hole in the top of each. Store the cards in a plastic bag hung on the board. Decorate the board and add the title "Penny's Garden."

Directions: Be sure the students know how to count sets from 1 to 10. Then discuss vegetables with them, finding out which the children like and those they don't like. Tell them they are going to help Penny count the vegetables in her garden. Have the children count the number of vegetables in each row in the garden and hang the correct numeral at the beginning of the row. Check the children's work.

Variations:

• Divide the bulletin board into several garden spaces and let a number of children work at a time.

• After the activity, have the children bring in real vegetables and make vegetable soup.

Worksheet: On the worksheet, the students count the number of fruits or vegetables in each picture and draw a line from them to the matching number.

Books to Read Aloud: If You Take a Pencil by Fulvio Testa; Ten LIttle Elephants by Robert Leydenfrost; How Many Kids Are Hiding on My Block? by Jean Merrill and Frances Gruse Scott; One Dancing Drum by Gail Kredenser.

Vegetable Patterns

Name_____

Count the number of vegetables in each picture. Draw a line from the picture to the correct number.

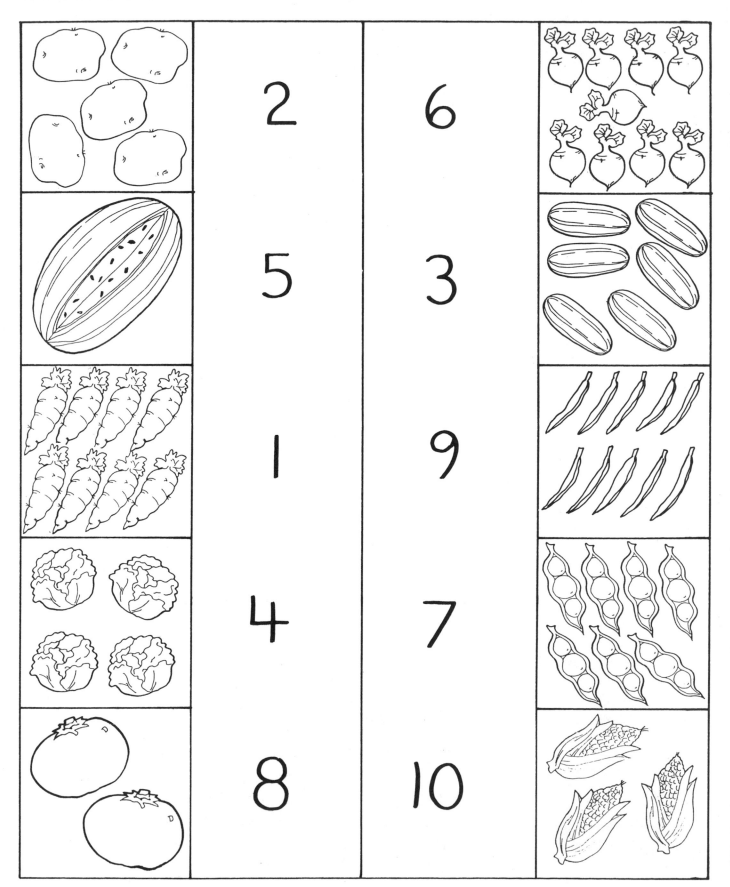

2

6

5

3

1

9

4

7

8

10

_____ 's **Homework**

Dear Parents,

   This activity will help your child practice counting. Discuss with your child all the kinds of fruits and vegetables you have in your house (fresh, canned, or frozen). Count the number of each and fill it in in the space below. Feel free to substitute different fruits or vegetables if you do not have the ones listed. Have your child return the completed paper to school.

I Can Count Fruits and Vegetables

Onions

Carrots

Canned corn

Potatoes

Beans

Radishes

Tomatoes

Apples

Bananas

Peaches

Plums

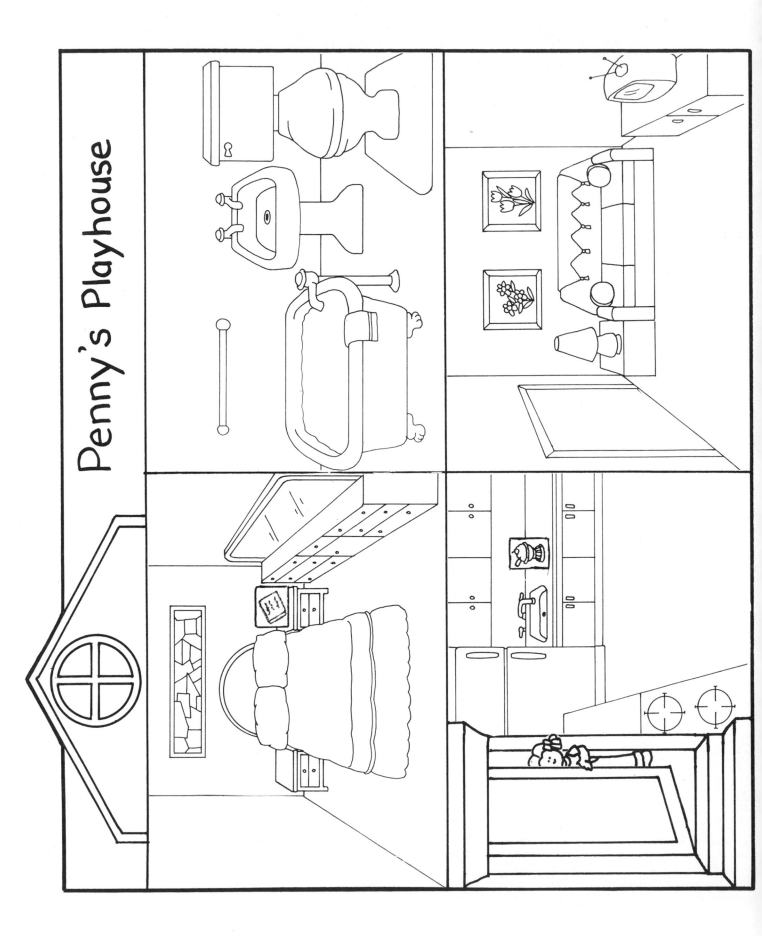

Penny's Playhouse

Activity 4: Penny's Playhouse

Objective: To classify familiar household items according to where each item is used

Materials: Patterns, construction paper, scissors, catalogs or old magazines, paste or glue stick, index cards, hole punch, stapler, pushpins, plastic bag, felt-tip pen, crayons

Construction: Enlarge and duplicate each of the room patterns. Cut out a suitable-size roof and any other additions you'd like to make to the house (front door, front yard with trees and flowers, clouds, etc.). Mount the patterns on the board to form a house (see the bulletin board page). Then cut out a variety of pictures of household items from catalogs or old magazines that are appropriate for the rooms of the house; some examples are telephones, wall clocks, dishwashers, rugs, chairs, and tables. Paste each picture onto an index card and punch a hole in the top. Laminate the cards and store them in a plastic bag hung on the board. Place pins on the board for hanging. Cut out and mount the title "Penny's Playhouse."

Directions: Tell the class that Penny's house is a mess. She needs the students to help her get all the things in her house back in their right places. Talk about the household items pictured on some of the cards and how they are used. Also discuss how some household items can be used in several different rooms in a house, for example, a telephone might be found in a bedroom and a kitchen and a chair might be found in the living room, the dining room, and the bedroom. Then have the children hang each picture in the bag in the appropriate room in Penny's house. Check the students' work, or have the children check each other's work.

Variations:

- Mount words about household items instead of pictures on the index cards. Let more advanced students read them and hang them up in the correct rooms.

- Adapt the activity to a folder format so that several children can work together.

Worksheet: The worksheet is a cut-and-paste activity. Have the students cut sight words from one page and paste them in the correct spaces on the other page.

Parent Letter: When the children have returned their work to class, have them add a roof to their house. Then display all the houses.

Books to Read Aloud: Things I Like by Margaret Wise Brown; What's On Your Plate? by Norah Smaridge; Pea Pod Doll House by Putnam Publishing Group; Let's Look All Around the House by Harold Roth; First Words: Home by Ed Emberley.

Room Patterns

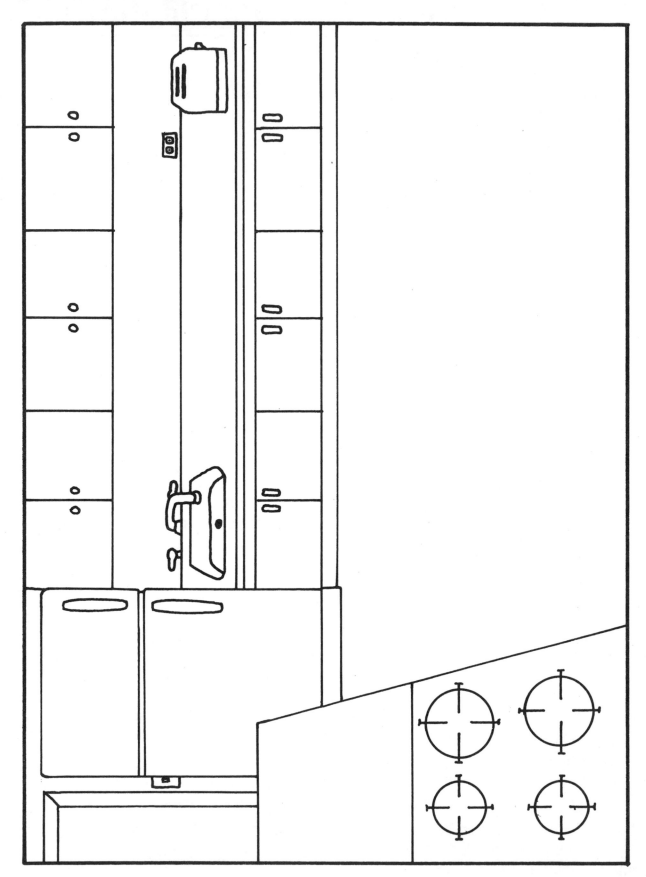

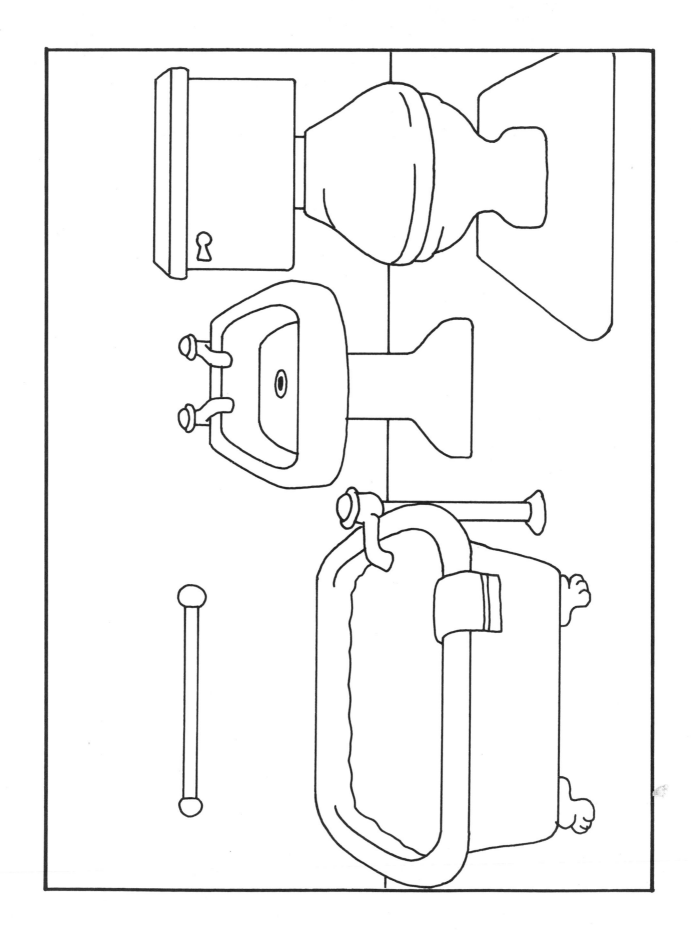

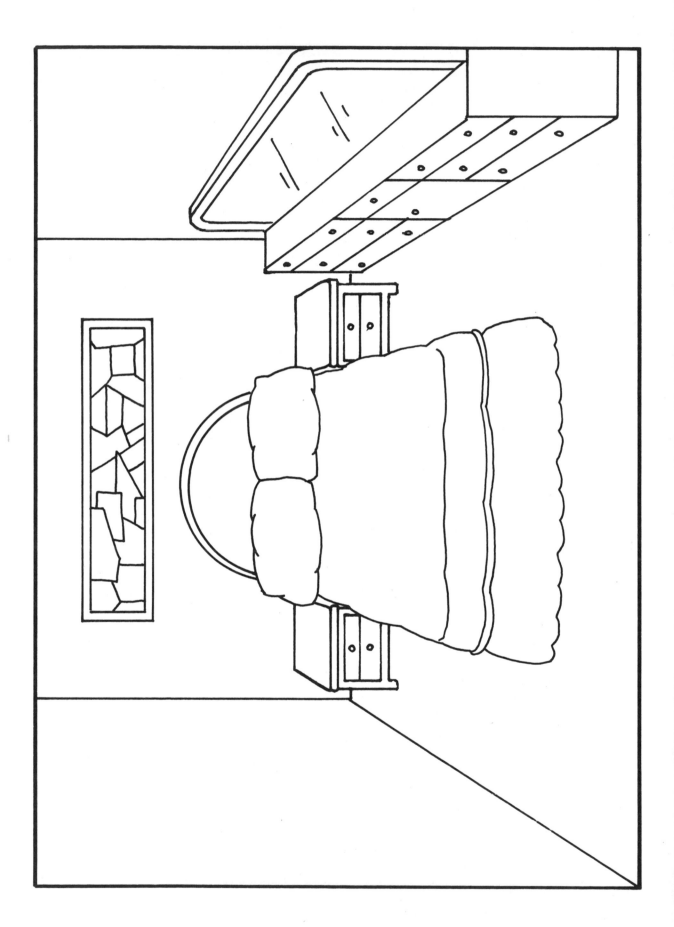

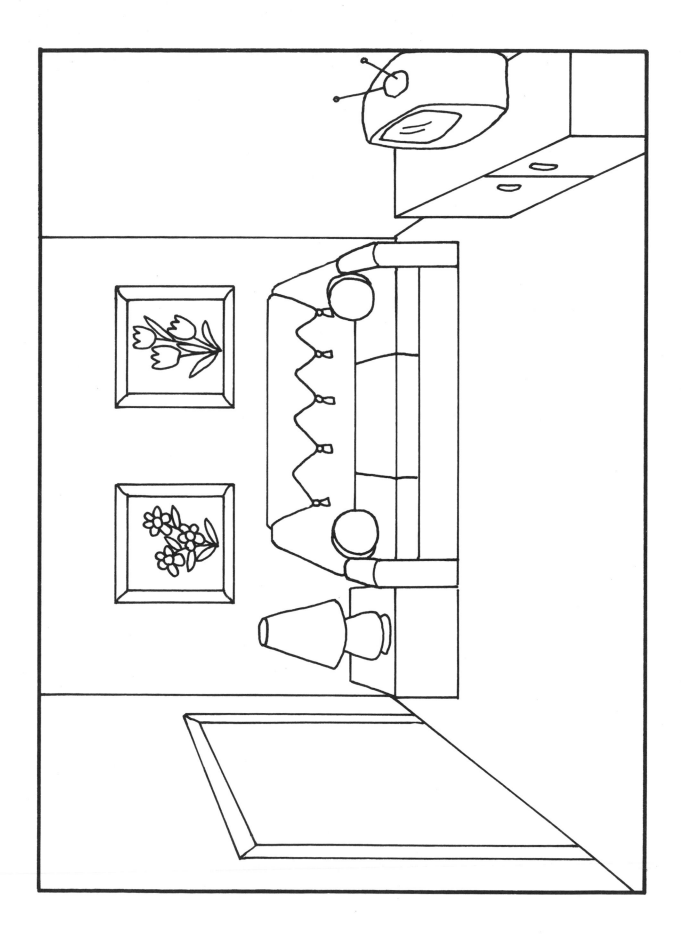

93

Name _____

Cut out the word cards on the next page. Paste each card in a box under the right group.

Word Cards

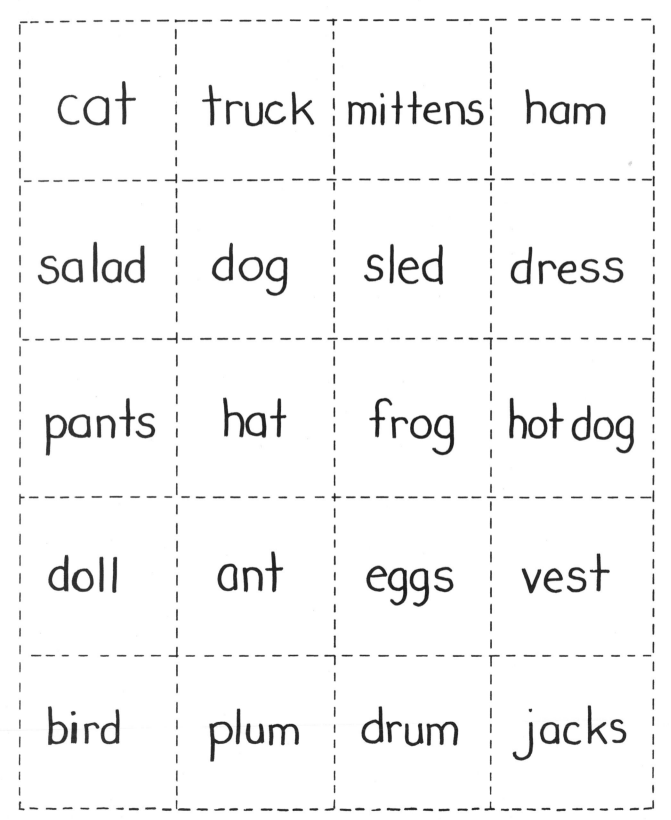

cat	truck	mittens	ham
salad	dog	sled	dress
pants	hat	frog	hot dog
doll	ant	eggs	vest
bird	plum	drum	jacks

Dear Parents,

    We are working at school on sorting items into groups. Please cut open a large brown bag or take a large piece of paper and divide it into four sections. Write the name of a room in the house—bathroom, living room, bedroom, and so on—in each section. Using old catalogs or magazines, cut out pictures of items that are appropriate for each room. Let your child decide on what should be cut out and where it should go. Then help your child paste the pictures onto the paper. Return the finished house to school.

This is Bashful Bear. Bashful Bear is a terribly shy teddy bear. The skills Bashful teaches through his bulletin board activities are:

1. Patterning
2. Size comparison
3. Vowel sounds
4. Color recognition

Bashful Bear
Pattern

Bashful

98

© 1990 Monday Morning Books, Inc.

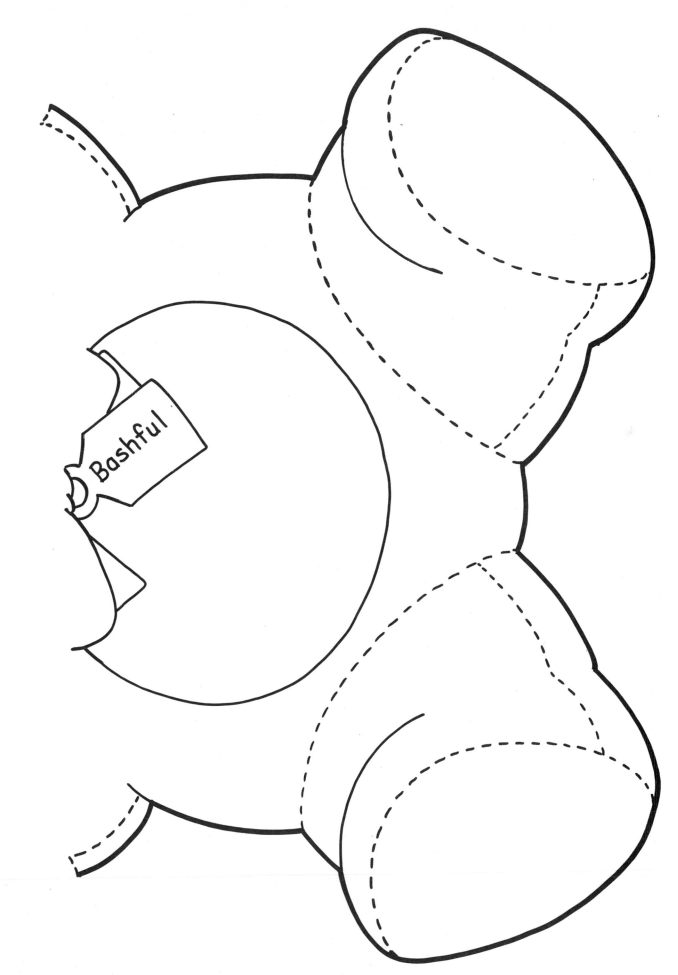

Bashful

Bears All in a Row

Activity 1: Bears All in a Row

Objective: To be able to recognize a pattern and add the next item in it

Materials: Patterns, scissors, construction paper, heavy-weight paper, stapler, pushpins, hole punch, plastic bag, paste or glue stick, crayons

Construction: Enlarge and duplicate the top half of the Bashful pattern and mount it on the board. Duplicate the bear strip patterns and mount them on heavy-weight paper. Color the bears as indicated on the patterns. Mount the strips on the board right below the Bashful pattern and place a pin at the end of each strip. Duplicate and cut out the bear answer cards that complete the patterns. Color them as indicated, then punch a hole in the top of each one. Laminate the cards and store them in a plastic bag hung on the board. Decorate the board and put up the title "Bears All in a Row."

Directions: Tell the students that Bashful Bear, the very shy teddy bear, is playing a patterning game. He wants the children to play the game with him. Point to one of the pattern strips on the board and chant the pattern so the children can hear the correct sequence: "Large, large, small, large, large, small." Point to and chant other patterns so the students realize that patterns can involve size, color, or position. Tell the students to figure out the pattern on each strip and hang the answer card that is the next step in the pattern. Go through the activity at least once as a group before having individual students or small groups work on it. If you use the activity early in the year, limit the pattern strips to only one variable, such as color. Check the students' work when completed.

Worksheets: The first worksheet is a cut-and-paste activity in which the students complete a pattern. The second worksheet, for older students, involves skip counting.

Books to Read Aloud: I Know An Old Lady by Colin Hawkins; Green Eggs and Ham by Dr. Seuss; Care Bears Up & Down by Peggy Kahn; Bumble B. Bear Cleans Up by Steven Cosgrove.

Bear Patterns

Pattern 1: Color red, blue, red, blue, red.

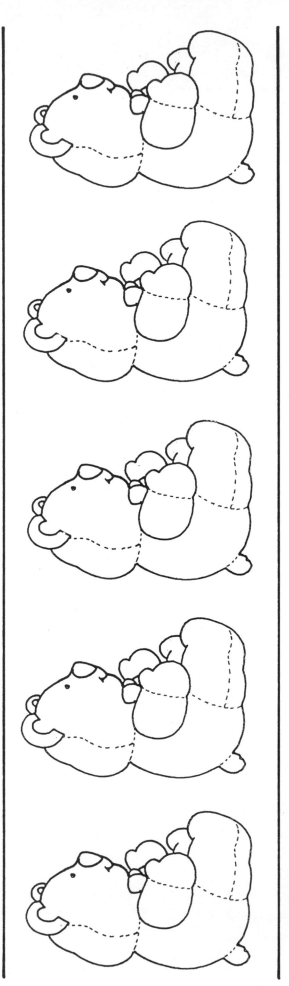

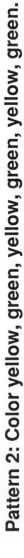

Pattern 2: Color yellow, green, yellow, green, yellow, green.

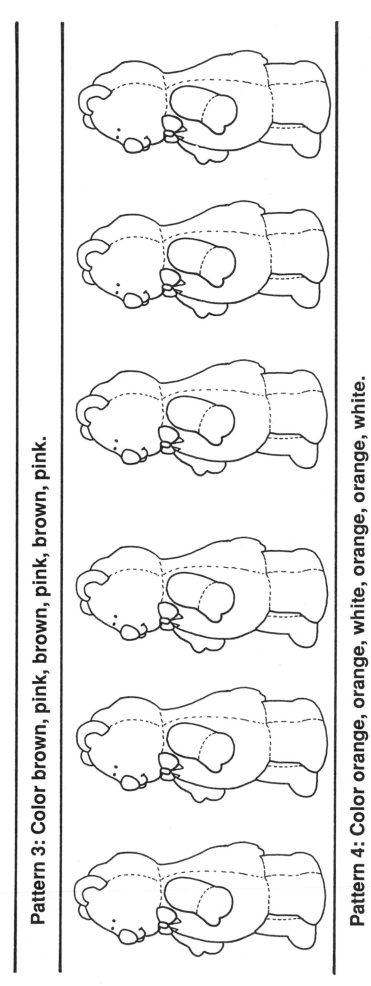

Pattern 3: Color brown, pink, brown, pink, brown, pink.

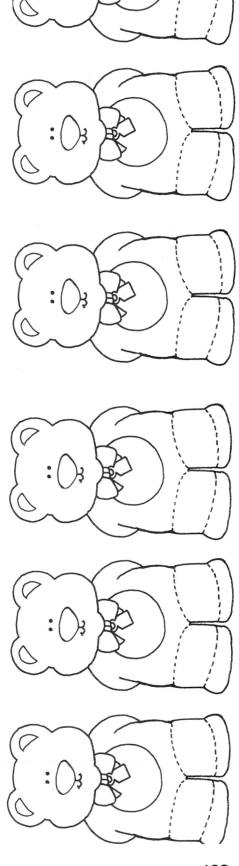

Pattern 4: Color orange, orange, white, orange, orange, white.

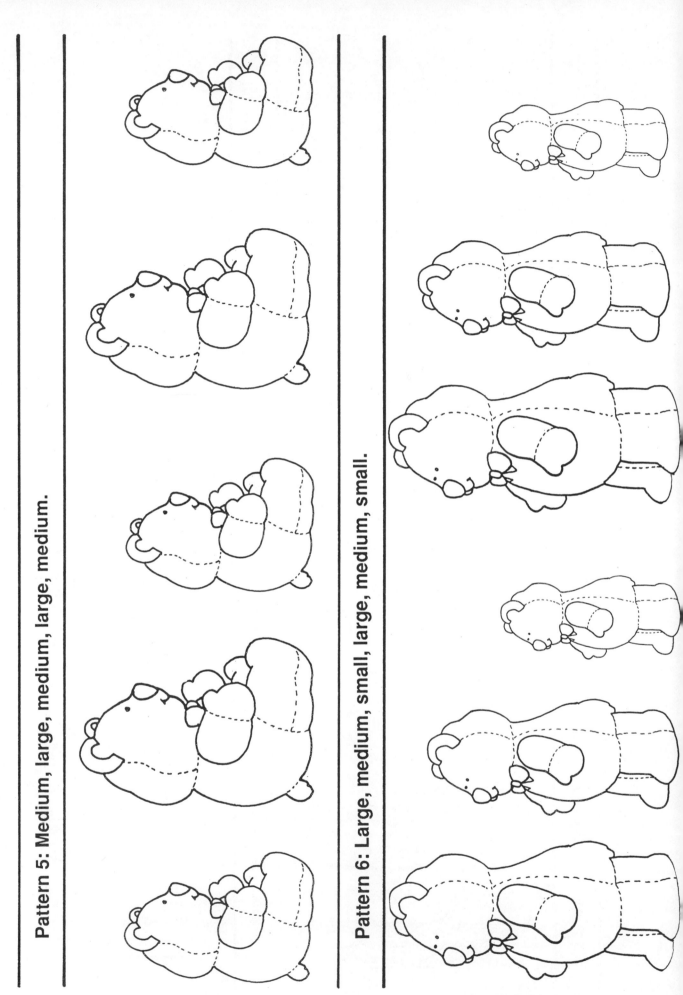

Pattern 5: Medium, large, medium, large, medium.

Pattern 6: Large, medium, small, large, medium, small.

Pattern 7: Side, front, side, front, side.

Pattern 8: Small, small, medium, small, small.

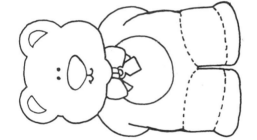

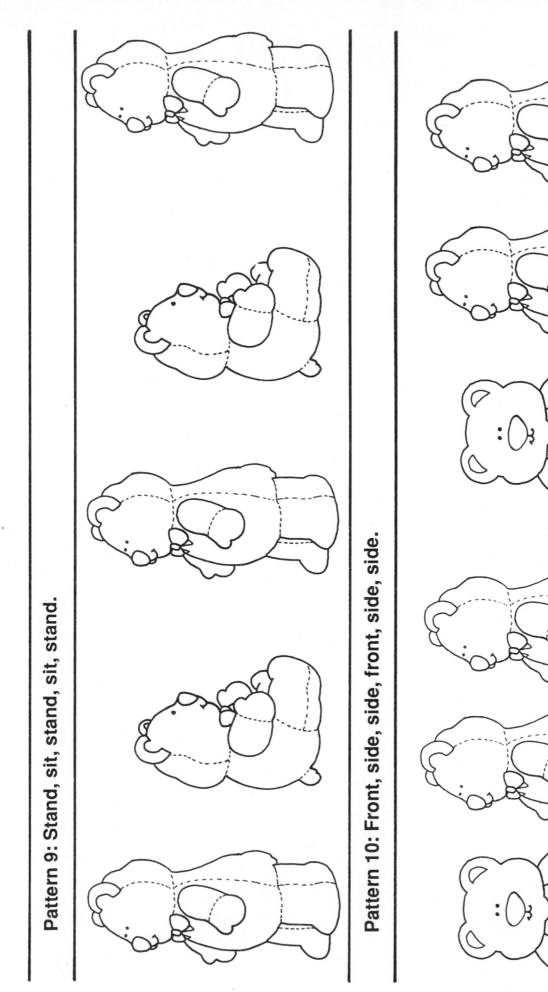

Pattern 9: Stand, sit, stand, sit, stand.

Pattern 10: Front, side, side, front, side, side.

Pattern 11: Large, large, small, large, large.

Pattern 12: Small, medium, large, small, medium, large.

Answer Cards

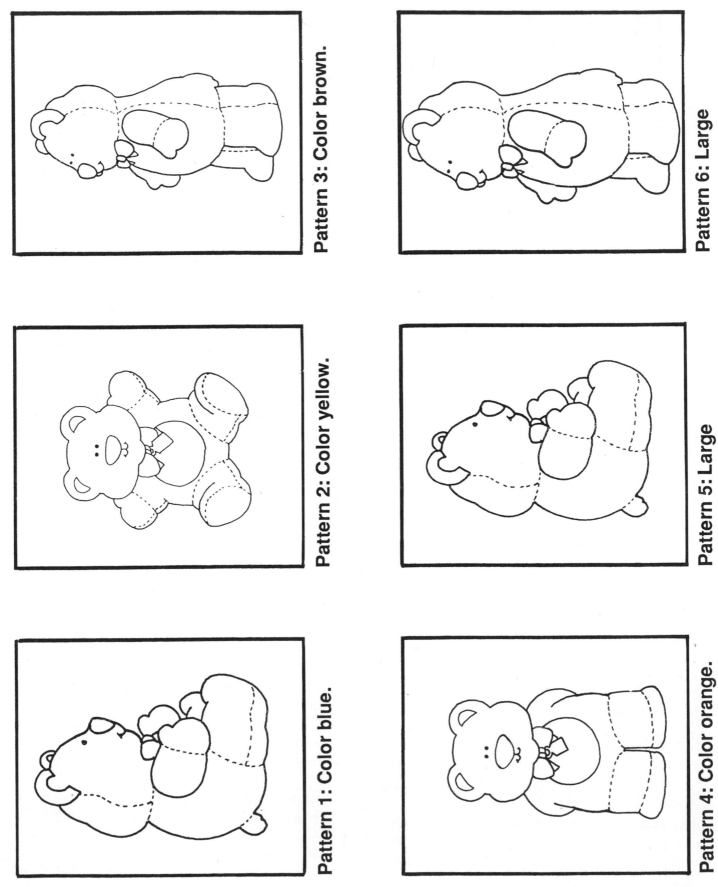

Pattern 3: Color brown.

Pattern 6: Large

Pattern 2: Color yellow.

Pattern 5: Large

Pattern 1: Color blue.

Pattern 4: Color orange.

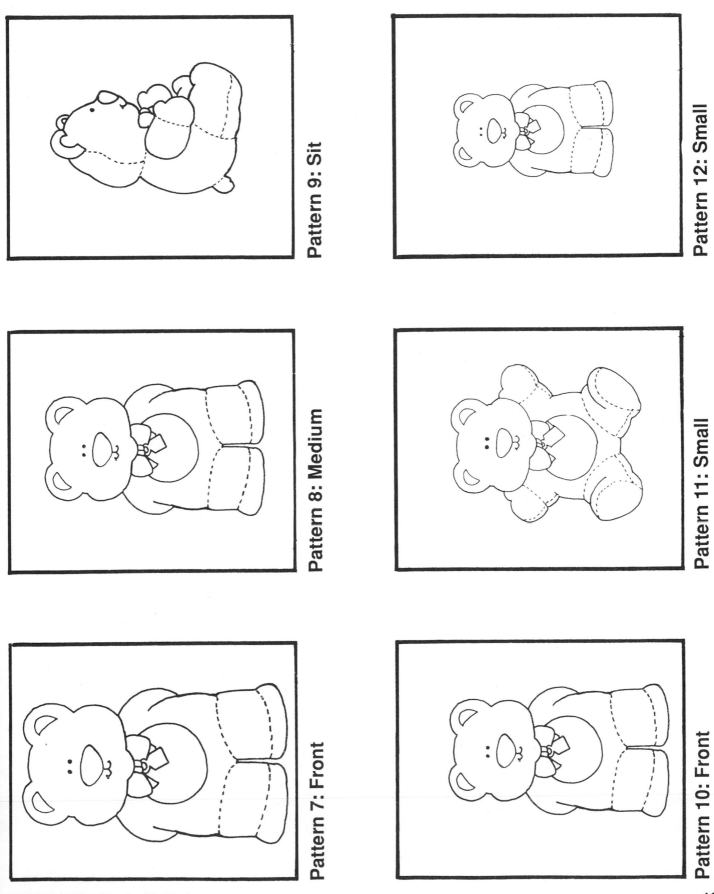

Pattern 9: Sit

Pattern 12: Small

Pattern 8: Medium

Pattern 11: Small

Pattern 7: Front

Pattern 10: Front

Name _____

Cut out a shape from the bottom of the page and paste it in the box to complete the pattern.

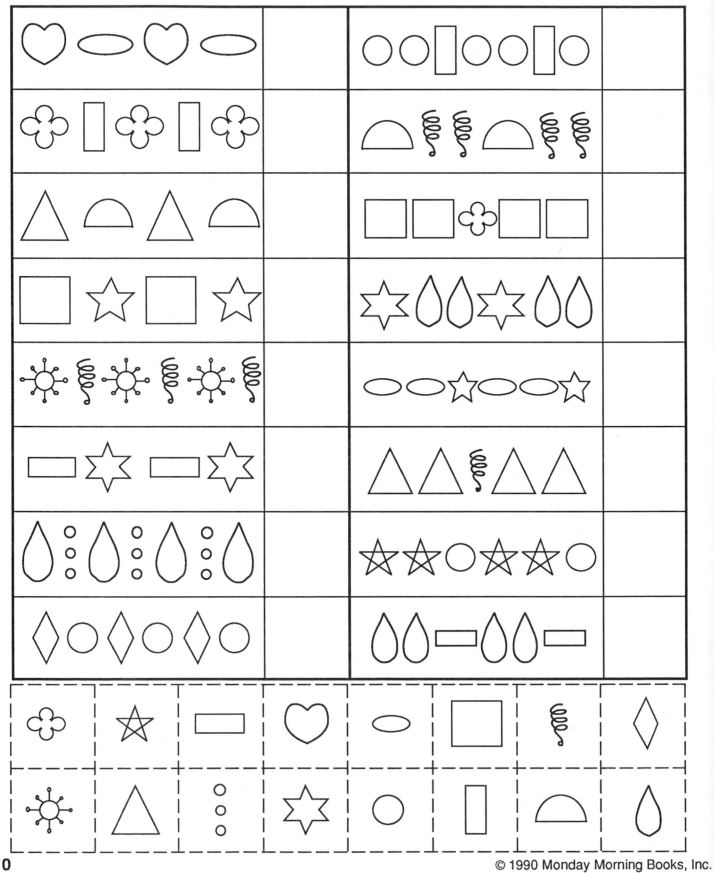

Name _____

| | 6 | | 12 | | 18 |

Skip count by 3.

| 5 | | 15 | | 25 | | 35 | | 45 |

Skip count by 5.

8   16   24

Skip count by 4.

| 2 | | 6 | | 10 | | 14 | |

Skip count by 2.

10   30   50

Skip count by 10.

12   24   36

Skip count by 6.

Dear Parents,

Our class is learning about patterning. Search in your cupboard for two or three of the following items: popcorn, macaroni, noodles, dried beans, or spaghetti. Use these items (break the spaghetti into inch-long pieces) to make two different patterns, for example, rice, popcorn, macaroni, rice, popcorn, macaroni. Glue the pattern pieces in the boxes marked "Parent's Sample." Then help your child match the patterns in the boxes marked "Child's Matching Pattern." Have your child return the patterning project to class.

Pattern 1 - Parent's Sample

Child's Matching Pattern

Pattern 2 - Parent's Sample

Child's Matching Pattern

Activity 2: Small, Medium, Large

Objective: To look at pictures of a variety of objects and determine if the objects are small, medium, or large

Materials: Patterns, scissors, construction paper, cloth pockets, stapler, push-pins, old magazines, index cards, paste or glue stick, plastic bag

Construction: Enlarge and duplicate a Bashful Bear pattern and mount it on the bulletin board. Duplicate and cut out a honey pot pattern; then use the pattern as a guide and make one larger honey pot cutout and another larger than that one. Attach a cloth pocket to each honey pot cutout. Then mount the honey pots on the board in small, medium, large order. Cut out pictures of objects that can easily be identified as small, medium, or large. For example, a picture of a feather and one of a pencil would work for small objects; a picture of a telephone and a kitten would be suitable for medium-sized objects; and a picture of a car and one of an elephant would work for large objects. Mount each picture on an index card. Laminate the cards and store them in a plastic bag hung on the board. Decorate the bulletin board and add the title "Small, Medium, Large."

Directions: Discuss with the students how some objects are very easy to pick up and other things cannot be picked up. Also talk about the fact that small things are often easily picked up, medium-sized things generally can be picked up with two hands, and large things often cannot be picked up at all. Tell the students that Bashful Bear needs help sorting some items according to size. Show the cards to the students and have them tell you if each picture shows something small, medium, or large. Then have the children sort the cards into the correct pockets. Check their work.

Variations:

• Duplicate and cut out four honey pots and label each with the name of one of the seasons. Mount pictures relating to the seasons on index cards and have the children sort the cards into the correct pockets.

• Mount two honey pots on the board, one labeled "Healthy Foods" and one labeled "Unhealthy Foods." Have the children sort pictures of food into the pockets.

Worksheet: The worksheet is a cut-and-paste activity in which the children classify items according to size.

Books to Read Aloud: Blue Sea by Robert Kahn; Size by Moira McLean; Shapes and Sizes by Richard Allington; All Shapes and Sizes by Shirley Hughes; Sesame Street Big Bird and Little Bird's Book of Big and Little from Golden Books.

Honey Pot Pattern

Name _____

Cut out the pictures and paste them under the right dog according to size.

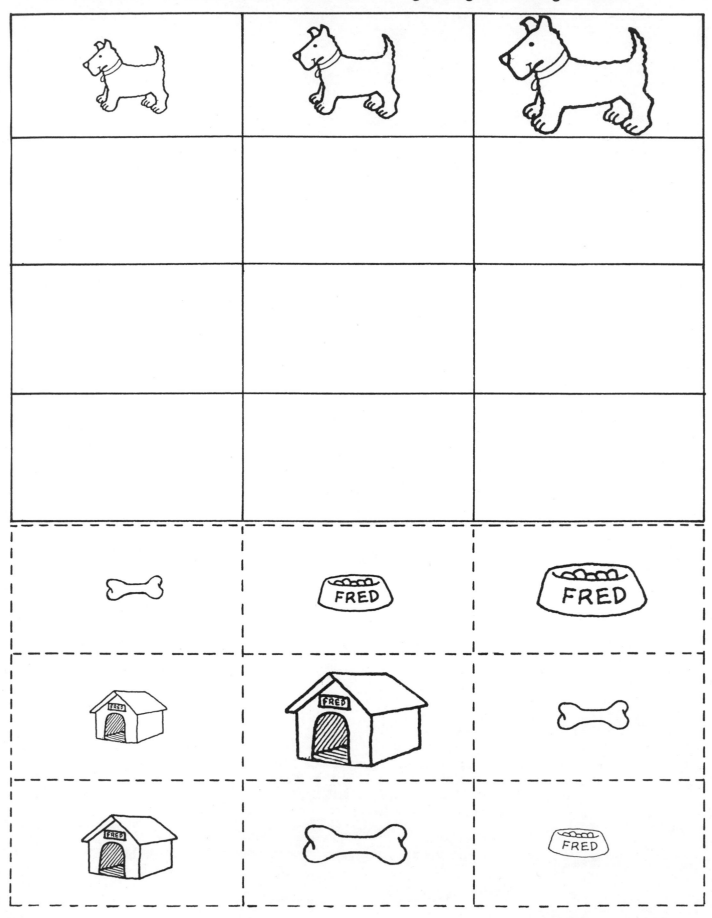

Dear Parents,

During our study of small, medium, and large, I would like you to emphasize these words and concepts. Please look around your house and find three of the same object in three different sizes. For example, you might locate three different sizes of adhesive bandages. Send these items to school marked with your name so they can be returned. To further reinforce the concept of small, medium, and large, have your child draw a flower in each of the boxes below that matches the size of the bee next to it.

Bashful Catches Butterflies

Activity 3: Bashful Catches Butterflies

Objective: To sort pictures by short vowel sounds

Materials: Patterns, scissors, construction paper, five small fishing nets, stapler, pushpins, old workbooks or magazines, paste or glue stick, plastic bag

Construction: Enlarge and duplicate the Bashful Bear pattern and attach it to the board. Label each fishing net with a different short vowel sound and mount the nets on the board. Duplicate and cut out five each of the butterfly patterns. Locate and cut out 15 pictures from old magazines, finding three pictures of items for each of the short vowel sounds. Glue each picture to a butterfly pattern. Laminate the butterflies and store them in a plastic bag hung on the board. Decorate the board and mount the title "Bashful Catches Butterflies."

Directions: Discuss the five short vowel sounds with the children and have them think of words that contain each sound. Let the children look through magazines and cut out pertinent pictures to glue on a wall chart of vowel sounds. Then tell the students that Bashful Bear likes to catch butterflies but he needs help putting each butterfly in the right net. Have the students help him by looking at each picture on the butterfly patterns, saying the short vowel sound in the word, and putting the butterfly into the correct net. Check the students' work and have them do over any incorrect responses.

Variations:

- Stencil a word on each butterfly pattern and have older students sort the words into the short vowel sound nets.

- Label one net with a plus sign, another with a minus sign. Write a math fact on each butterfly pattern but omit the plus or minus sign. Have the students sort the patterns into the correct net.

- Have the students make butterfly collages using scraps of construction paper. Display the finished works during parent-teacher conferences or in a prominent place in the school.

Worksheet: The worksheet asks students to fill in the missing vowel in short vowel sound words.

Books to Read Aloud: The Butterfly Book by Cynthia Overbeck.

Butterfly Patterns

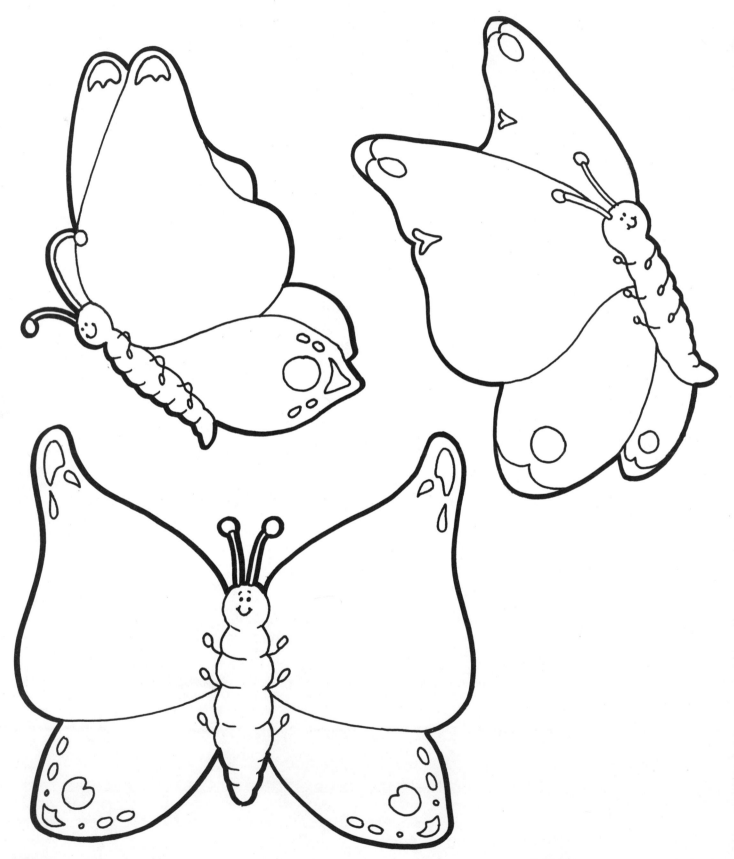

Name _____

Fill in the missing vowel: a, e, i, o, or u.

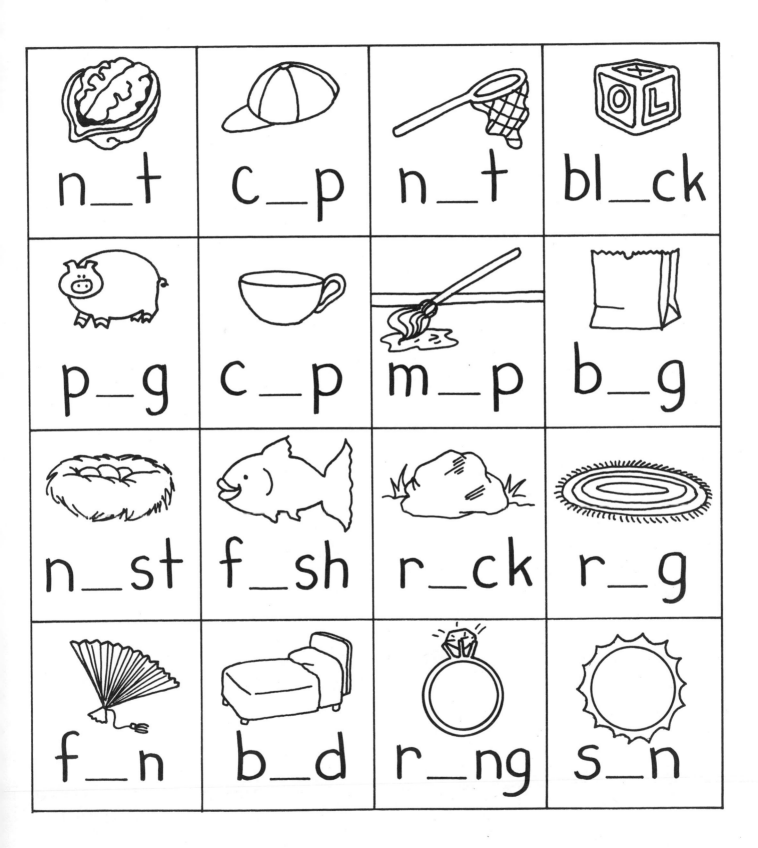

n_t   c_p   n_t   bl_ck

p_g   c_p   m_p   b_g

n_st   f_sh   r_ck   r_g

f_n   b_d   r_ng   s_n

_____'s **Homework**

Dear Parents,

　　We are learning about vowel sounds at school. Please go over the pictures below with your child and talk about the vowel sound in each object. Help your child find and circle the three pictures in each row that go with the long vowel sound at the beginning of the row. Have your child return the completed sheet to class.

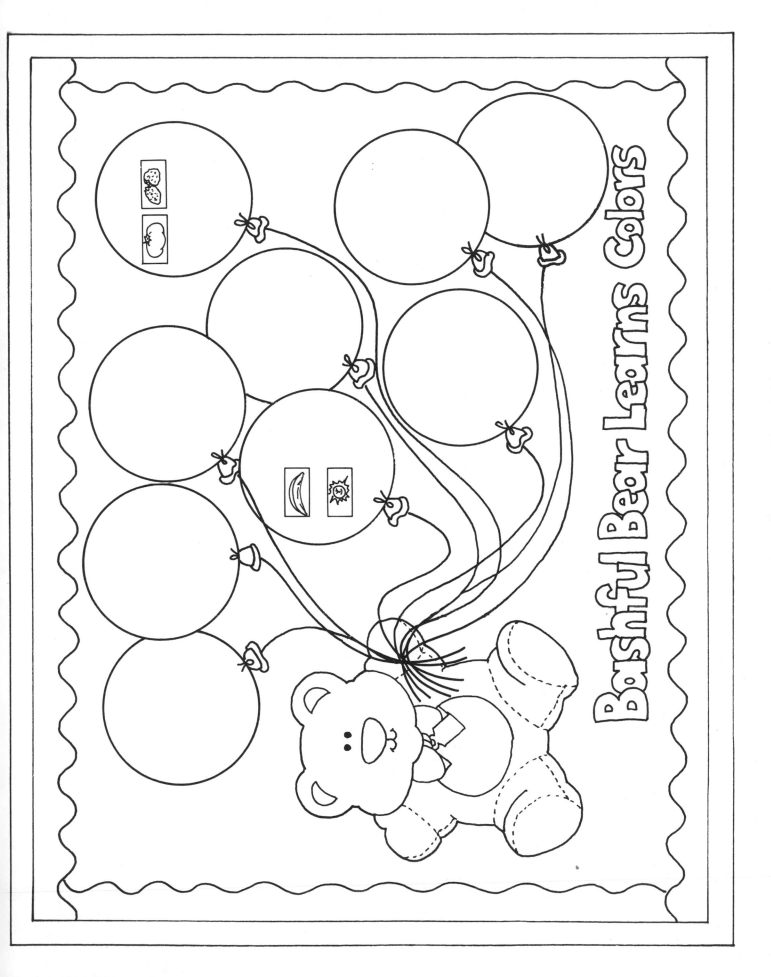

Bashful Bear Learns Colors

Activity 4:
Bashful Bear Learns Colors

Objective: To be able to sort items according to the colors the items should be

Materials: Patterns, scissors, construction paper, white paper, yarn or felt-tip pen, hole punch, stapler, pushpins, plastic bag

Construction: Enlarge and duplicate the Bashful Bear pattern and mount it to one side of the board. Cut out a large balloon shape from each of the following construction paper colors: red, black, purple, white, green, yellow, brown, orange, and blue. Laminate the balloons and mount them on the bulletin board. Place several pins in each balloon. String yarn or draw a line between each balloon and Bashful's front paws. Then copy the object patterns onto white paper and cut them apart. Laminate the patterns and punch a hole in the top of each one. Store them all in a plastic bag hung on the board. Decorate the board and add the title "Bashful Bear Learns Colors."

Directions: Discuss the different balloon colors and talk about things that belong in each color group. Tell the children that they will be helping Bashful Bear sort a number of objects into the correct color group. Have the students take each card out of the plastic bag and think about its color. Then have them hang each card on the correct color balloon. Check the students' work.

Variation: Collect as many items shown on the patterns, plus any others you think of, and put them in a pillowcase "feely bag." Let each student reach in and try to guess what an item is just by feeling it.

Worksheet: The students will need to listen to and follow your directions to complete the worksheet page.

Parent Letter: The homework assignment will be very enjoyable if it is done outdoors in the fall or spring.

Books to Read Aloud: Green Says Go by Ed Emberley; Harlequin and the Gift of Many Colors by Remy Charlip; Shapes and Colors by Jeanne Schwartz; Red, Yellow, Blue: A Wrinkles Book of Colors by Steve and Anita Shevett.

Object Patterns

Name _____

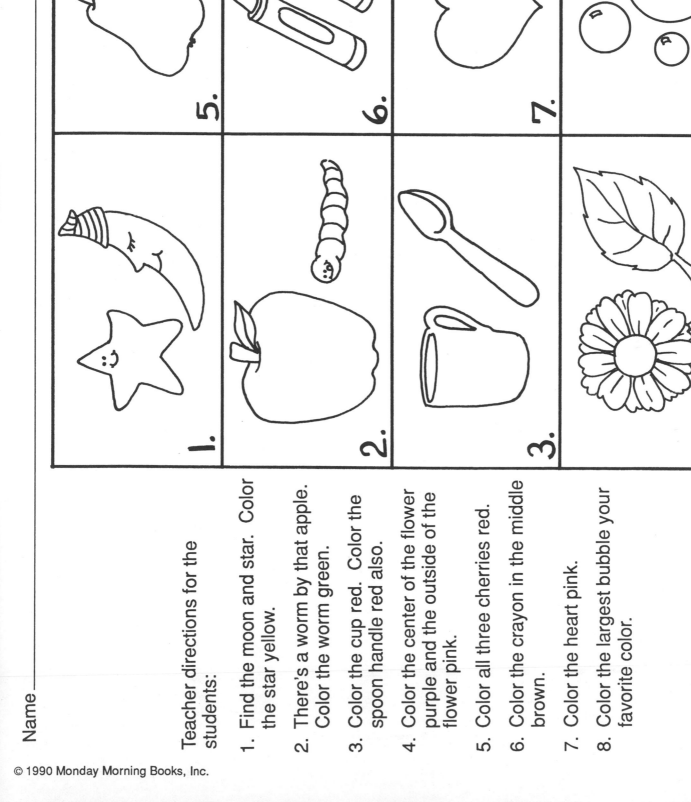

Teacher directions for the students:

1. Find the moon and star. Color the star yellow.

2. There's a worm by that apple. Color the worm green.

3. Color the cup red. Color the spoon handle red also.

4. Color the center of the flower purple and the outside of the flower pink.

5. Color all three cherries red.

6. Color the crayon in the middle brown.

7. Color the heart pink.

8. Color the largest bubble your favorite color.

_____'s **Homework**

Dear Parents,

   We are working on color recognition in school. Please take a walk with your child (outdoors or in) and focus on all the different colors you see. Then have your child tape or draw the items you saw in the appropriate space on the color wheel below. If no items for a certain color were seen, leave that space blank. Send the completed page to school with your child.

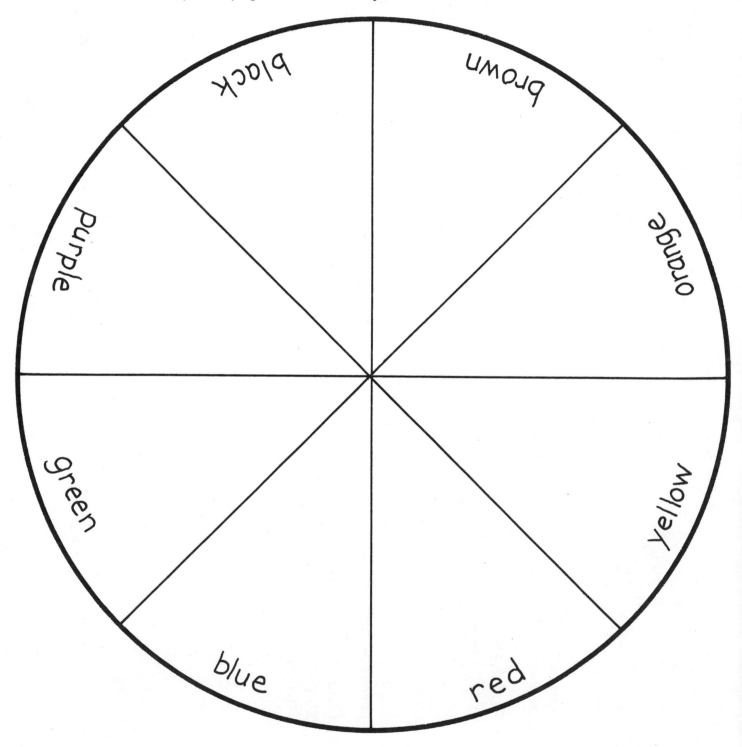